AS-Level
Psychology
AQA A

The Revision Guide

Editors:
Rachel Selway, Dominic Hall, Andy Park.

Contributors:
Richard Carciofo, Martin Chester, Charley Darbishire, Chris Dennett, Christine Johnson, Tracey Jones, Asraf Sattar, Denise Say, Emma Singleton.

Proofreaders:
Sue Hocking, Teresa Jamieson, Christine Johnson.

Published by Coordination Group Publications Ltd.

ISBN-10: 1 84146 989 0
ISBN-13: 978 1 84146 989 8

Groovy website: www.cgpbooks.co.uk
Jolly bits of clipart from CorelDRAW®
Printed by Elanders Hindson Ltd, Newcastle upon Tyne.

Contents

*We deliberately haven't put any answers in this
book, because they'd just be saying what's in
the revision guide. So instead, here's how to
write answers, and do well.*

Short-Term and Long-Term Memory

I used to worry that I could remember where I was in, say, May '84, but I couldn't recall why I'd just walked into a room. But it's due to the difference between short-term and long-term memory. Or something... I forget the exact reason.

Memory is a **Process** Where Information is **Retained** About the Past

Memories are thought to have a physical basis or '**trace**'. Most psychologists agree that there are three types of memory, **sensory memory (SM)**, **short-term memory (STM)** and **long-term memory (LTM)**.

SM is visual and auditory information that passes through our senses very briefly. SM disappears quickly through **spontaneous decay** — the trace just fades. SM isn't around for very long, so most studies are on LTM and STM.

> **STM and LTM differ in terms of:**
> 1)   **Duration** — How long a memory lasts.
> 2)   **Capacity** — How much can be held in the memory.
> 3)   **Encoding** — Transferring information into code, creating a 'trace'.
>
> STM has a **limited capacity** and a **limited duration** (i.e. we can remember a little information for a short time).
>
> LTM theoretically has an **unlimited capacity** and is theoretically **permanent** (i.e. lots of information forever).

Research Has Been Carried Out into the Nature of **STM and LTM**

Peterson and Peterson (1959) Investigated STM Using Trigrams

Peterson & Peterson (1959) investigated the duration of STM.

Method:	Participants were shown **nonsense trigrams** (3 random consonants e.g. CVM) and asked to recall them after either 3, 6, 9, 12, 15 or 18 seconds. They then had to count backwards in 3s between seeing the trigrams and recalling them. This was an '**interference task**' — it prevented them repeating the letters to themselves.
Results:	After **3 seconds**, participants could recall about **90%** of trigrams correctly. After **18 seconds**, only about **2%** were recalled correctly.
Conclusion:	When rehearsal is prevented, **very little** can stay in STM for longer than about **18 seconds**.
Evaluation:	Nonsense trigrams are artificial, so this study lacks **ecological validity**— the results might not apply to real life settings. Meaningful or 'real life' memories may last longer in STM.

Bahrick et al. (1975) Investigated LTM in a Natural Setting

Bahrick et al. (1975) studied VLTMs (very long term memories).

Method:	392 people were asked to list the names of their ex-classmates. (This is called a '**free-recall test**'). They were then shown photos and asked to recall the names of the people shown (**photo-recognition test**) or given names and asked to match them to a photo of the classmate (**name-recognition test**).
Results:	Within 15 years of leaving school, participants could **recognise** about **90%** of names and faces. They were about **60%** accurate on **free recall**. After 48 years, recognition was still good, at about **75%**, but free recall had declined to about **30%** accuracy.
Conclusion:	The study shows evidence of **VLTMs** in a '**real life**' setting. Recognition is better than recall, so there may be a huge store of information, but it's not always easy to **access** all of it, i.e. all the information's there, you just need help to get to it.
Evaluation:	This study showed better recall than other studies on LTM, but this may be because **meaningful** information is stored better. However in a 'real life' study like this, it's hard to **control** all the variables, making these findings less reliable — there's no way of knowing exactly **why** information was recalled well.

Other studies have also looked at VLTMs. Waganaar and Groeneweg (1990) found that 30 years after being imprisoned in concentration camps, people could still remember extensive details from their experience.

Short-Term and Long-Term Memory

STM and LTM Have Very *Different Capacities*

Jacobs (1887) studied the capacity of STM.

Method:	Participants were presented with a string of letters or digits. They had to repeat them back in the same order. Initially, there were 3 digits, then 4, etc, until the participant failed to recall the sequence correctly.
Results:	Participants recalled, on average, about **9 digits** and about **7 letters**. This capacity increased with **age** up to a point.
Conclusion:	Based on the range of results, Jacobs concluded that STM has a **limited storage capacity** of **5-9 items**. Individual differences were found, such as STM increasing with age, possibly due to increased brain capacity or memory techniques, such as **chunking** (see below). Digits may have been easier to recall as there were only 10 to remember, compared to 26 letters.
Evaluation:	This research is **artificial**, so more meaningful information may be recalled better, perhaps showing STM to have an even greater capacity.

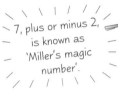 *7, plus or minus 2, is known as 'Miller's magic number'.*

Miller (1956) reviewed research into the capacity of STM. He found that people can remember about seven items. He argued that the capacity of STM is **seven, plus or minus two**. He also suggested that we use 'chunking' to combine individual letters or numbers into larger more meaningful units. So 2,0,0,3,1,9,8,7 is about all the digits STM can hold. 'Chunked' into the meaningful recent years of 2003 and 1987, it's much easier to remember. In fact, STM could probably hold about seven such pieces of chunked information (2003, 1987, 1999, 2001...), increasing STM's capacity.

Encoding is About the Way Information is Stored in Memory

In **STM**, we try to keep information active by repeating it to ourselves. This means it generally involves **acoustic** coding. In **LTM**, encoding is generally **semantic** — it's more useful to code words in terms of their meaning, rather than what they sound or look like (although encoding in LTM **can** also be visual or acoustic).

Encoding of memories can be visual (pictures), acoustic (sounds, e.g. 'dog' and 'dot' are acoustically similar) or semantic (meanings, e.g. 'dog' and 'canine' are semantically similar).

Baddeley (1966) investigated encoding in STM and LTM.

Method:	Participants were given four sets of words, either **acoustically similar** (e.g. man, mad, mat), **acoustically dissimilar** (e.g. pit, cow, bar), **semantically similar** (e.g. big, large, huge) or **semantically dissimilar** (e.g. good, hot, pig). Participants were asked to recall them either immediately or following a 20-minute task.
Results:	If recalling the word list immediately (therefore from **STM**), participants had problems recalling acoustically similar words. If recalling after an interval (from **LTM**), they had problems with semantically similar words.
Conclusion:	The patterns of confusion between similar words suggest that **LTM** is more likely to rely on **semantic** encoding and **STM** on **acoustic** encoding.
Evaluation:	There are other types of LTM (e.g. episodic memory, procedural memory) which this experiment doesn't consider.

Practice Questions

Q1 Describe two differences between STM and LTM.
Q2 Define encoding, capacity and duration.
Q3 Describe the findings of one study of STM.

Exam Questions

Q1 Compare STM and LTM in terms of capacity, duration and encoding. [6 marks]

Q2 Describe and evaluate studies into the duration of STM and LTM. [18 marks]

Remember the days when you didn't have to remember stuff like this...

How long you remember something depends on how much it means to you personally. So trivial things that are going to have no bearing whatsoever on your life are quickly forgotten. But more important stuff tends to stay in your head a whole while longer. Not sure if that makes this stuff easy or hard to learn — but try to remember it for more than twenty minutes.

Models of Memory

This page is all about why you can't remember the last page. Maybe you didn't rehearse it enough, or maybe you only looked at the letters instead of trying to understand the facts. Or maybe you spilt tea on it and can't read the words...

Atkinson and Shiffrin (1968) Created the **Multi-Store Model**

The multi-store model is made up of three memory stores — a **sensory store**, a **short-term store** and a **long-term store**. Information from the environment initially goes into **sensory memory**. If you pay attention to it, or think about it, the information will pass into **short-term memory**. Some information may be processed further (you might rehearse it to yourself, for example), and will therefore be transferred to **long-term memory**.

Support for the model

1) The **Primacy Effect** — Research shows that participants are able to recall the first few items of a list better than those from the middle. The model explains this because **earlier** items will have been **rehearsed** better and transferred to **LTM**. If rehearsal is prevented by an interference task, the effect disappears, as the model predicts.

2) The **Recency Effect** — Participants also tend to remember the last few items better than those from the middle of the list. Earlier items are rehearsed, so transfer to LTM, whilst **later** items are recalled because they're still in **STM**.

3) People with **Korsakoff's Syndrome** (amnesia developed due to chronic alcoholism) provide support for the model. They can recall the **last** items in a list (unimpaired recency effect), suggesting an unaffected **STM**. However, their **LTM** is very poor. This supports the model by showing that STM and LTM are **separate stores**.

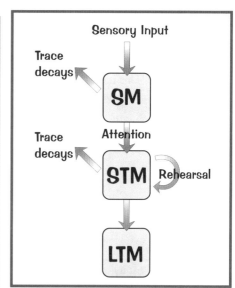

Limitations of the model

1) In the model, information is transferred from STM to LTM through **rehearsal**. But in **real life**, people don't spend time rehearsing, but they do transfer information into LTM. Rehearsal is not always needed for information to be stored and some items can't be rehearsed e.g. smells.

2) The model is **oversimplified**. It assumes there is only one long-term store and one short-term store. This has been disproved by evidence from **brain damaged** patients, suggesting several **different** short-term stores, and other evidence suggesting different long-term stores.

Baddeley and Hitch (1974) Developed the **Working Memory Model**

Baddely and Hitch developed a multi-store model of STM called the 'working memory model'. It has **3 parts**:

1) The **central executive** can be described as attention. It has a limited capacity and controls two 'slave' systems that also have **limited capacity**, which are:

2) The **visuo-spatial sketchpad** (STM for visual and spatial information).

3) The **articulatory-phonological loop** (holds speech-based information). It contains a **phonological store** (the inner ear) and an **articulatory process** (the inner voice).

Studies using '**interference tasks**' support the model — if participants are asked to perform two tasks using the same system at once, their performance will be affected, e.g. saying 'the the the' while silently reading something is very difficult. Both these tasks use the articulatory-phonological loop, which has limited capacity — it can't cope with both tasks, so performance on one, or both, will be affected.

Shallice and Warrington (1974) found **support** for the model through their case study of KF. **KF** was a brain damaged patient who had an impaired STM. His problem was with immediate recall of words presented **verbally**, but not with visual information. This suggested he had an impaired **articulatory loop**, therefore providing evidence for the working memory model's view of STM.

A potential criticism is that the idea of a central executive is **simplistic** and **vague**.

Models of Memory

Craik and Lockhart (1972) Developed the *Levels of Processing Model*

Craik and Lockhart's levels of processing model focuses on the processing of incoming information.

They discussed three levels of processing called **physical processing**, **phonemic processing** and **semantic processing**:

1 **Physical processing** occurs at a 'shallow' level and analyses information in terms of its **physical** qualities, e.g. **a word is typed in black ink.**

2 **Phonemic processing** occurs at a '**deeper**' level than physical processing. It focuses on the **sound** of information, e.g. **pea rhymes with bee.**

3 **Semantic processing** occurs at the '**deepest**' level and analyses the **meaning** of information, e.g. **a pea is a vegetable.**

The levels of processing theory suggests that information **processed** at a **deeper** level should be **recalled** better.

As the idea of deep and shallow processing was thought to be a bit **simplistic**, Craik and Lockhart included ideas of **elaboration**, **organisation** and **distinctiveness**.

They predicted that information will be recalled better if it has been **elaborated** (e.g. explained more, perhaps with examples), or **organised** (e.g. if participants had to sort information into categories), or made **distinctive** (e.g. said with a funny voice).

They found **support** for their model.

Craik and Tulving (1975) also did a series of experiments to support the model. They found that words processed **semantically** were recalled best, **phonemically** second best and **physically** worst.

The theory has been **criticised**:

1) There is a **circular argument** over what **depth** really is. In this model, the definition of good recall is something that comes from deep processing. The definition of deep processing, though, is something that leads to good recall. However, with elaboration, organisation and distinctiveness added to the model, this criticism doesn't work so well.

2) The model ignores the **distinction** between STM and LTM.

3) The model may also be confusing **effort** with **depth**.

Practice Questions

Q1 What is the recency effect?
Q2 How many components does the working memory model consist of and what are they?
Q3 Give two criticisms of the levels of processing model.
Q4 Give two criticisms of the working memory model.

Exam Questions

Q1 Describe the levels of processing model. [6 marks]

Q2 Compare and contrast the multi-store memory model and the working memory model. [18 marks]

Memory, all alone in the moonlight... something about the moon... la la la...

I don't know about you, but I find these pages pretty boring. Kind of learnable, but still boring enough that you find yourself face-down on your desk in a pool of dribble, with a biscuit stuck to your forehead. Don't fret anyway, it's not long before you can start learning about the gory experiments with electric shocks and nastiness. Much better than this stuff...

SECTION ONE — COGNITIVE PSYCHOLOGY

Forgetting

Forgetting is great — such an easy way to not answer difficult questions. Just screw your eyes up, point your head towards the sky, wibble and say 'Ooh, I know it, it's in there, err, I can't remember'.

Forgetting is When Learnt Information Can't Be Retrieved

Experiments on memory assume that if you can't retrieve a memory, it's forgotten. Forgetting is thought to happen when information is **unavailable** in **STM** and **inaccessible** and/or **unavailable** in **LTM**. In other words, we can forget because:

1)   The information was never **stored** — an **availability** problem, e.g. you didn't pay attention when the information was presented.

2)   The information was stored, but is hard to **retrieve** — an **accessibility** problem, e.g. you read something once, a long time ago, and now need a lot of help to recall it.

3)   The information is **confused** — there is an **interference** problem, e.g. two pieces of learnt information are too similar, and you can't tell them apart easily.

Decay and Displacement are Theories Explaining Forgetting in STM

Theories suggest that information in STM might either just disappear with time, or get pushed out by new information:

Trace Decay Theory

Memories have a physical basis or '**trace**'. This trace **decays** over time unless it is passed to LTM. This explains the findings from the **Peterson and Peterson (1959)** experiment — when rehearsal of information was prevented, very little information stayed in STM for longer than about 18 seconds (see page 2).

However, we can't be sure that the trace really decayed instead of being overwritten by new information (**displacement**).

Reitman (1974) gave participants words to learn, then made them listen for a tone as an interference task, preventing rehearsal. There was no new information to push out the old. So if recall was impaired this would suggest the reason was decay, not displacement. There was a slight, but not huge, reduction in recall so we have some evidence for decay.

Displacement Theory

Displacement theory suggests that new information physically overwrites old information. **Waugh and Norman (1965)** found that with lists of digits, participants were much better at recalling digits from near the **end** of the list than near the beginning. This supports displacement theory.

However, they did a similar experiment with the digits presented at different **speeds**. They found that recall improved when digits were presented faster, which suggests that **decay** rather than displacement was to blame.

Seeing as there is evidence for both the decay and displacement theories of forgetting in STM, a possible explanation could be that **both** are true. There is no reason why **decay and displacement** can't both cause forgetting in STM.

Forgetting in LTM Could Be Caused By a Lack of Availability

An argument of **decay** or **interference** can be applied to **LTM**. However, in LTM, studies have found more problems in recall if you take in new information rather than just having a relatively information-free break. Therefore, **interference** is a more likely explanation than decay, as new information affects the recall of old information.

Interference can be retroactive or proactive.

Retroactive interference is where **new** information interferes with the ability to recall **older** information.

Proactive interference is where **older** information interferes with the ability to recall **new** information. This interference can be removed, though, if useful information is given as a prompt (a **cue**). (This explanation has been criticised as it suggests forgetting is better explained as **retrieval failure**, and it doesn't easily explain forgetting in the **real world**.)

Other factors influence forgetting.

We have more chance of retrieving the memory if the **cue** is **appropriate**. Cues can be **internal** (e.g. your **mood**) or **external** (e.g. **context**, like surroundings, situation, etc). We remember more if we are in the same **context / mood** as we were in when we encoded the information originally. This is known as **cue-dependent learning**.

Forgetting

Tulving and Psotka Investigated Forgetting in LTM

Tulving and Psotka (1971) — forgetting in LTM

Method: Tulving and Psotka compared the theories of **interference** and **cue-dependent forgetting**.

Each participant was given either 1, 2, 3, 4, 5 or 6 lists of 24 words. Each list was divided into 6 categories of 4 words. Words were presented in category order, e.g. all animals, then all trees etc.

After the lists were presented, in one condition, participants had to simply recall all the words — **total free recall.**

In another condition, participants were given all the category names and had to try to recall words from the list – **free cued recall**.

Results:
1) In the **total free recall** condition, there was strong evidence of **retroactive** interference. Participants with 1 or 2 lists to remember had higher recall than those with more lists to remember, suggesting the later lists were **interfering** with remembering the earlier lists.

2) In the **cued recall** test, the effects of retroactive interference **disappeared**. It didn't matter how many lists a participant had, recall was still the same for each list (about **70%**).

Conclusion: The results suggest that interference had not caused forgetting. Because the memories became accessible if a cue was used, it showed that they were available, but just inaccessible. Therefore, the forgetting shown in the total free recall condition was **cue-dependent forgetting**.

Evaluation: Cue-dependent forgetting is thought to be the best explanation of forgetting, as it has the **strongest** evidence. Most forgetting is seen to be caused by **retrieval failure**. This means that virtually all memory we have is available in LTM, we just need the right cue to be able to access it. However, the evidence is **artificial** (e.g. recalling word lists), lacking meaning in the real world. Also, it would be difficult, if not impossible, to test whether all information in LTM is accessible and available, and just waiting for the right cue.

Jasper couldn't quite recall what his mother had told him about these things.

Practice Questions

Q1 Give two explanations of forgetting in LTM.
Q2 Outline two explanations of forgetting in STM.
Q3 What is meant by cue-dependent forgetting?
Q4 Outline the main features of displacement theory.

Exam Questions

Q1 Outline and evaluate two explanations of forgetting in LTM. [6 marks]

Q2 Outline and evaluate one theory of forgetting in STM. [6 marks]

Remember, remember the 5th of October...

This is a great page for playing psychologist. You can easily make up lists of words and then get your friends to read them. Give them an interference task and then test them. What fun. I love psychology experiments. I'm always doing experiments on my friends, though they've gone off the idea a bit since that incident with the misplaced electrode.

The Role of Emotional Factors in Memory

*Emotion affects memories. In fact, interestingly enough, highly emotional material can be either **more** memorable or **less** memorable. These pages are all about how nobody really knows why...*

'Flashbulb Memories' Are Really Vivid Memories of Emotional Events

Brown and Kulik (1977) noticed that people were able to **recall vividly** what they were doing when highly important and dramatic events occurred, such as the assassination of President Kennedy.

1) Recent events that probably caused flashbulb memories include September 11th and Princess Diana's death.
2) Flashbulb memories don't have to be **negative** — they can be about dramatic **positive** events too, e.g. Gainsborough Trinity winning the FA cup. OK, it hasn't happened yet, but if it did, I'd remember it vividly...
3) They are almost as if a **photograph** is taken at the time and stuck on the memory.
4) They are **enduring** and **accurate**.
5) They seem to **contradict** the idea that thorough processing in STM is required for a memory to become an LTM.
6) Flashbulb memories support the idea that **emotional factors** and **distinctiveness** are important in memory.
7) Brown and Kulik thought that a special **mechanism** in the **brain** must be responsible for flashbulb memories.

Other Researchers Suggested Theories on Flashbulb Memories

Many researchers have put forward different theories to explain the **cause** and **reliability** of flashbulb memories.

Cahill and McGaugh (1998) suggested that adrenaline is involved.

1) They argued it wouldn't be useful to remember everything as we'd just be overloaded with information.
2) What would be useful, though, would be a biological mechanism that could **regulate** what we remember by deciding the **importance** of events.
3) They argued that when our emotions are highly **aroused**, we produce the hormone **adrenaline**, which has 2 effects:
   a) In the **short-term**, it makes us **ready** to respond to the situation.
   b) In the **long-term**, it affects our **memory**, helping us remember important situations, and affecting our responses to similar situations in the future.
4) When rats were injected with a stimulant drug with a similar effect to adrenaline, they learnt a new task much faster than normal. This supports the theory.

Since the highly emotional and dramatic event, Emma had more things to worry about than her flashbulb memory.

McCloskey et al (1988) studied the reliability of flashbulb memories.

1) Shortly after the explosion of the space shuttle Challenger, they asked participants for their memories of the event.
2) They retested them nine months later and found that there were some **discrepancies** between the original and later recall.
3) This suggests that flashbulb memories are also subject to **forgetting**.

Conway et al (1994) disagreed with McCloskey et al.

1) They felt the Challenger explosion was **not** a **significant** enough event in peoples' lives.
2) They interviewed people in various countries a few days after Margaret Thatcher's surprising and important resignation, then again at a later date.
3) They found **86%** of the UK participants to have flashbulb memories after 11 months, compared to **29%** in other countries.
4) They argued that an event with a distinctive **meaning** is more **memorable**. Margaret Thatcher's resignation would be more **meaningful** to people in the UK than to people in other countries, making it also more memorable.

Sheingold and Tenney (1982)

They found adults could recall events that caused significant **emotion**, for example, the birth of a child. This was a **retrospective** study (looking back at events from the past). The problem with it is that we don't know about the original events, so it's hard to check the accuracy of their recall.

The Role of Emotional Factors in Memory

Repression *is the* Motivated Forgetting *of Uncomfortable Memories*

Freud (1915) said that 'repression' was a way of protecting the ego (conscious mind) from uncomfortable memories. Anything that might be traumatic is removed from conscious thought through **motivated forgetting**. So traumatic memories are more likely to be forgotten than happy ones. In fact, anything that has been forgotten could have been repressed, because it is always possible that unconsciously, we were uncomfortable with it.

It is hard to **prove** this theory, but **Herman and Schatzow (1987)** found that **28%** of women who had experienced incest in childhood had memory deficits and evidence of **repression**. Other studies also **support** the theory:

Williams (1994) found evidence of repression.

Method:	129 girls who were admitted to hospital in 1970 due to a sexual assault were interviewed 17 years later.
Results:	**38%** of the women had **no recall** of the original incident. Of those who did remember, **16%** said they had at one time been unable to recall the event, but then recovered their memory. Women who were **younger** at the time of the assault or who knew those who had abused them were more likely to forget.
Conclusion:	The findings **support** the theory of repression, but also suggest that **recovery** occurs.
Evaluation:	This was a very **biased** sample (almost entirely poor urban women), so there could be another reason for the poor recall. Perhaps the original accounts were **fictitious**, or perhaps later in life, the women were just **unwilling** to talk about such personal matters.

Bradley and Baddeley (1990) found that **emotionally arousing** words (e.g. fear) were more **difficult** to retrieve than emotionally neutral words (e.g. cow), but they could still be retrieved in time. They concluded that emotional arousal or anxiety causes **repression** but that this effect **lessens** with time.

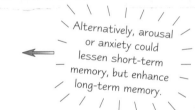
Alternatively, arousal or anxiety could lessen short-term memory, but enhance long-term memory.

Myers and Brewin (1994)

Method:	The length of time it took participants to recall **negative** childhood memories was measured for 'repressors' and other personality types. 'Repressors' are people who deal with anxiety by being **defensive** — they have low levels of anxiety, but high levels of defensiveness.
Result:	Repressors took **longer** to recall negative childhood memories than other personality types, but also had more **early** negative memories and reported more **difficult** relationships with their parents.
Conclusion:	The findings suggest that individuals with more **anxiety-inducing** memories are more likely to become repressors in order to **repress** these negative childhood memories.
Evaluation:	Again, this may reflect an **unwillingness** to recall rather than repression.

Practice Questions

Q1   Explain the term 'flashbulb memory'.
Q2   What type of events can lead to 'flashbulb memories'?
Q3   What is repression?
Q4   What did Myers and Brewin discover about repression?

Exam Questions

Q1   Explain how emotion can inhibit memory.   [6 marks]

Q2   Discuss how emotion can enhance memory.   [6 marks]

I'm so unhappy, but I can't remember why...

There seems to be evidence for repression, but you'd think that if it was entirely true, we'd all have forgotten September 11th and other horrific events. But no, we've got really vivid memories of those. Well, I'm confused. What makes one awful thing more likely to be remembered and another more likely to be forgotten? I have no idea, ask someone else...

Critical Issue: Eyewitness Testimony

If you witness a crime or an accident, you have to report what you saw, and your version of events could be crucial in prosecuting someone... But your memory isn't as accurate as you might think...

Eyewitness Testimony Can Be **Inaccurate** and **Distorted**

Eyewitness testimony (EWT) is the **evidence** provided by people who **witnessed** a particular event or crime. It relies on **recall** from memory. EWT includes, for example, **descriptions** of criminals (e.g. hair colour, height) and crime scenes (e.g. time, date, location).

Loftus and Palmer (1974) investigated how EWT can be **distorted**.
They used **leading questions**, where a certain answer is subtly implied in the question:

Loftus and Palmer (1974) studied eyewitness testimony.

Method: Participants were shown films of a multiple car crash. They were then asked questions including 'How fast do you think the cars were going when they **hit**?' In different conditions, the word 'hit' was replaced with '**smashed**', '**collided**', '**bumped**' or '**contacted**'. A week later, they were asked if they had seen any broken glass. (There was no broken glass in the films.)

Results: Participants who were asked the speed when the cars '**smashed**' reported **higher** speeds than participants in the other conditions. More participants in the '**smashed**' condition also claimed to have seen **broken glass**.

Conclusion: **Leading questions** can affect the **accuracy** of people's memories of an event.

Evaluation: This has implications for questions in **police interviews**. However, this was an artificial experiment — watching a video is not as **emotionally arousing** as a real life event, which potentially affects recall. In fact, a later study found that participants who thought they'd witnessed a **real** robbery gave a more **accurate** description of the robber.

Loftus and Zanni (1975) also considered **leading questions**. They showed participants a film of a car accident, then asked them either 'Did you see **the** broken headlight?' or 'Did you see **a** broken headlight?'. There was no broken headlight, but **7%** of those asked about '**a**' broken headlight claimed they saw one, compared to **17%** in the group asked about '**the**' broken headlight. So, the simple use of the word 'the' is enough to affect the accuracy of people's memories of an event.

Facial Recognition is Also Important in EWT

Witnesses often have to try and recall the **individual facial features** of a criminal so that police can try and make an **identikit** image. There is debate, however, over the **reliability** of these images based on research into how we normally identify faces:

Young et al (1987) studied memory of faces.

They found that people recognise faces better using the face as a **whole** rather than individual features. This has important **implications** as **identikit** pictures used by the police are based on individual features rather than how the face holds together as a whole.

Bruce and Valentine (1988) investigated motion in faces.

They attached lights to faces and filmed them in the dark. They found participants watching the movements of the lights could often identify the **emotion** and sometimes recognise the **person** just by the movements of the face. Police **identikit** pictures, however, are just motionless faces, so do not tap a large volume of facial knowledge.

Bruce and Young (1986) studied mechanisms of facial recognition.

They studied brain damaged patients, and suggested that recognition of **unfamiliar** faces relies on **feature** detection (eyes, nose, etc.), as in identikit pictures, whereas recognition of **familiar** faces relies on recognition of the **configuration** of the whole lot. This therefore lends **support** for the use of police identikit images, because presumably identikit images are of strangers.

Critical Issue: Eyewitness Testimony

Reconstructive Memory is About Filling the Gaps in Memory

1) **Bartlett** believed that when we remember something, we only store **some** elements of the experience.
2) We **reconstruct** events using these elements, filling in the **gaps** in the memory with our own **schema**.
3) Schema are **ready-stored opinions** and **expectations** which we use for quick judgements to deal with the world.
4) Our **culture**, **beliefs**, **prejudices** and **previous experiences** all help build our schema.
5) For example, a '**granny schema**' might be that all grannies have white curly hair, like knitting, and say 'haven't you grown'. Of course, not all grannies do, but you might use this granny schema to fill in the gaps in the vague memory you had of someone's granny.

Bartlett (1932) demonstrated reconstructive memory.

Method: Participants were shown a short story from a different culture, which therefore contained **unfamiliar** material. After a number of days, participants were asked to **recall** the story.

Results: The recalled stories were always **shorter** than the original. Many parts were recalled from the participants' own cultural perspectives, with certain facts **changed** to fit. For example, 'canoe' was changed to 'boat'. The recalled version soon became very **fixed** over time with only minor variations.

Conclusion: The **meaning** of a story is remembered, but the gaps are filled in with more familiar material to make the story **easier** to remember. This has an effect of **skewing** information to make it fit our schema.

Comment: It is possible that errors occurred from **conscious guessing** rather than participants actually believing that their recalled stories were the same as the original. Later studies have found that if participants were told from the beginning that **accurate recall** was required, errors dropped significantly.

Sulin and Dooling (1974) found support for Bartlett's findings.

Method: A story was read to participants, who were told it was about either Gerald Martin (a fictional person) or Adolf Hitler. They were then given a few sentences and asked whether they came from the text. Some sentences didn't come from the text, but were concerned with well-known facts about Hitler.

Results: Participants who thought the story was about Hitler were more likely to claim the key sentences were in the text.

Conclusion: Participants' previous knowledge (schema) **distorted** their recall, as in Bartlett's study.

Schemas are Used During Both Encoding and Reconstruction

1) The way information is **initially perceived** and **stored** is affected by schema and stereotypes.
2) Research shows that people can be mistaken in their initial **encoding** of events, leading to mistaken recall.
3) So schemas and stereotypes are used when **forming** a memory as well as when trying to **reconstruct** a memory.

Practice Questions

Q1 What are schemas?
Q2 What are eyewitness testimonies?
Q3 Describe the study by Loftus and Palmer.
Q4 Describe the main findings of Bartlett's 1932 study.

Exam Questions

Q1 Describe research on face recognition. What do these findings show us about EWTs? [18 marks]

Q2 Outline Bartlett's research on reconstructive memory and explain why this is significant in EWTs. [18 marks]

A tall thin man, quite short, with black, fair hair — great fat bloke she was...

Well, now I haven't a clue what I've really experienced in my life. Did that man I saw shoplifting really have stubble, scars, a pierced chin and a ripped leather jacket, or is that just my shoplifter-stereotype kicking in? In fact, come to think of it, I couldn't actually tell you whether my granny has a hairy chin or not. I think she does, but then I think all grannies do...

The Development of Attachments

An 'attachment' is a strong, emotional bond between two people.
Psychologists are interested in how and when our first attachments form and what influences them.

Schaffer *Identified the Following Stages in Attachment Formation:*

1) The **pre-attachment phase** — During the first **two to three months** of life, the baby learns to **separate** people from objects but doesn't have any strong preferences about who cares for it.

2) The **indiscriminate attachment phase** — Between **three and seven months** it starts to clearly **distinguish** and **recognise** different people, smiling more at people it knows than at strangers. However, there are still no strong preferences about who cares for it.

3) The **discriminate attachment phase** — From **seven months onwards** it becomes able to form **true, emotionally strong attachments** with **specific** people. This is shown by being content when that person is around, distressed when they leave and happy when they return. It may be scared of strangers and avoid them.

4) The **multiple attachment phase** — From about **nine months** it can form **attachments to many people**. Some attachments may be stronger than others and have **different functions**, e.g. for play or comfort, but there doesn't seem to be a limit to the number of attachments it can make.

Schaffer and Emerson (1964) — evidence for stages of attachment

Method: 60 babies were observed in their homes in Glasgow every four weeks from birth to about 18 months. Interviews were also conducted with their families.

Results: Schaffer's stages of attachment formation were found to occur. Also, at 8 months of age about 50 of the infants had more than one attachment. About 20 of them either had no attachment with their mother or had a stronger attachment with someone else, even though the mother was always the main carer.

Conclusion: Infants form attachments in **stages** and can attach to **many people**. **Quality of care** is important in forming attachments, so infants may not attach to their mother if other people are more sensitive or loving.

Comment: There is now a lot of evidence to support Schaffer and Emerson's results and the proposed stages of attachment formation, but there are also criticisms of the study. For example, Schaffer and Emerson used a **limited sample** and the evidence from interviews and observations may be **biased** and **unreliable**.

Additionally, there are some cross-cultural differences that should be considered. **Tronick et al (1992)** found that infants in Zaire had a strong attachment with their mother by six months of age but didn't have strong attachments with others, even though they had several carers.

Different Factors **Influence** *the* **Development** *of* **Attachments**

1) The **age** of a child may be important. Some researchers, such as **John Bowlby** (see page 15), have claimed that attachments should develop before a certain age (e.g. 3-5 years), otherwise they will never properly develop.

2) The **quality of care** that a child receives may be crucial for forming attachments. Just being around a child may not be enough — parents need to be caring and sensitive to its needs (this is shown in Schaffer and Emerson's results).

3) A child's **temperament** may make it easier or harder for them to form attachments, regardless of the quality of care that they receive. Some aspects of temperament may be inborn.

There are many ways to form a strong attachment with your child.

The Development of Attachments

An Infant's **Reaction** in a **Strange Situation** Shows if it's **Securely** Attached

Ainsworth et al (1978) — The Strange Situation

Method:	12-18 month old infants were left in a room with their mother. Different scenarios occurred — a stranger approached, the infant was left alone, the mother returned. The infant's reactions were constantly observed.
Results:	About 20% of infants were **'anxious-avoidant' (type A)** — they ignored their mother and didn't mind if she left. A stranger could comfort them. About 65% were **'securely attached' (type B)** — content with their mother, upset when she left, happy when she returned and avoided strangers. About 15% were **'anxious-resistant' (type C)** — uneasy around their mother and upset if she left. They resisted strangers and were also hard to comfort when their mother returned.
Conclusion:	Infants showing different reactions to their carers have different types of attachment.

The findings above have been shown many times in the USA, but it was not known whether they could be applied to other cultures. Cross-cultural studies have since been carried out:

Van Ijzendoorn and Kroonenberg (1988) — cross-cultural studies

Method:	The findings from 32 studies of 'the strange situation' in different countries (e.g. Japan, Britain, Sweden, etc) were analysed to find any overall patterns.
Results:	The percentages of children classified as Type A, B or C were very **similar** in the countries tested.
Conclusion:	There are cross-cultural similarities in raising children, producing common reactions to 'the strange situation'.

There are Important **Findings** from Strange Situation Research

1) **Attachment type may influence later behaviours.** Securely attached children may be more confident in school and form strong, trusting adult relationships. 'Avoidant' children may have behaviour problems in school and find it hard to form close, trusting adult relationships. 'Resistant' children may be insecure and attention seeking in school and, as adults, their strong feelings of dependency may be stressful for partners.

2) **Some cultural differences are found. Grossman et al (1985)** claimed that more 'avoidant' infants may be found in Germany because of the value Germans put on independence — so 'avoidance' is seen as a good thing.

3) **The causes of different attachment types are debatable**.
The causes may be the sensitivity of their carers and/or their inborn temperament.

4) **The strange situation experiment doesn't show a characteristic of the child**. The experiment only shows the child's relationship with a specific person, so they might react differently with different carers, or later in life.

Practice Questions

Q1 Outline Schaffer's stages of attachment formation.
Q2 Explain some of the factors that influence attachment formation.
Q3 Explain the differences between type A, B and C attachments.
Q4 What have cross-cultural studies shown about attachments?

Exam Questions

Q1 Describe research on the development of attachments. [6 marks]
Q2 Outline the 'Strange Situation' experiment. [6 marks]

Try and get all these theories of attachment firmly stuck in your head

Next time you're in trouble at college and your parents are called in to 'discuss your behaviour', try sobbing gently under your breath, 'I think it's all my anxious-resistant attachment formation, it's left me insecure and needy of attention'. It's a desperate attempt, but it might just make your parents feel bad enough to let you off.

Explanations of Attachment

These pages deal with the five different psychological explanations for how and why attachments develop between infants and their carers. Simple eh — you'd think, but this is psychology...

Psychodynamic Theory Offers an Explanation for Attachment Formation...

Sigmund Freud claimed we are born with a part of personality called the **'id'** (the animal bit).

The id is only concerned with our **biological needs** — it demands food when we're hungry, makes us sleep when we are tired, etc.

A baby will cry when it needs something, like when it's hungry. Its mother will then feed it and this will give the baby pleasure because the need is removed. So the baby will make a **link** between having its mother around and having its biological needs for food, warmth, etc fulfilled. This is why babies 'attach' to their mother.

...As Does **Behaviourist Theory**

Like Freud's theory, the behaviourist theory focuses on the baby wanting its needs fulfilled.
However, the behaviourist theory of **conditioning** gives a more precise explanation for how attachments form:

Classical Conditioning. This is about learning **associations** between different things in our environment. Getting food naturally gives the baby **pleasure**. The baby's desire for food is fulfilled whenever its mother is around to feed it. So an **association is formed between mother and food**. So, whenever its mother is around the baby will feel pleasure — i.e. 'attachment'.

Operant Conditioning. **Dollard and Miller (1950)** claimed that babies feel discomfort when they're hungry and so have a desire to get food to **remove the discomfort**. They find that if they cry, their mother will come and feed them — so the discomfort is removed (this is **'negative reinforcement'**). The mother is therefore associated with food and the baby will want to be close to her — because if the mother is close, food will be too. This produces 'attachment behaviour' (distress when separated from the mother etc).

Behaviourists have shown that we can learn by **making associations** — so this could easily apply to forming attachments, and food is a very obvious reinforcement.

However, even though babies do spend most of their time either eating or sleeping, it doesn't mean that they automatically attach to the person who feeds them.

In fact, **Schaffer and Emerson (1964)** found that many babies did not have strong attachments with their mothers, even though she fed them. **Good quality interaction with the baby seemed more important** — the baby will attach to whoever is the most sensitive and loving (see page 12). This is also shown in Harlow's study of monkeys:

Harlow (1959) showed the need for 'contact comfort'.

Method: Experiments were undertaken where rhesus monkeys were raised in isolation. They had two 'surrogate' mothers. One was made of wire mesh and contained a feeding bottle, and the other was made of cloth but without a feeding bottle.

Results: The monkeys spent most of their time clinging to the cloth surrogate and only used the wire surrogate to feed. The cloth surrogate seemed to give them **comfort** in new situations.

Conclusion: The monkeys needed **'contact comfort'** as much as food and would attach to the source of this comfort, not the source of food. This **contradicts** the Freudian and behaviourist focus on feeding as the cause of attachment.

Comment: The results of this experiment might not apply to humans, seeing as it used monkeys. Additionally, isolating monkeys is not a very **ethical** method of studying attachment development.

Mummy?

Explanations of Attachment

We're Not Done Yet — There's the Ethological Approach...

Ethology is the study of animals in their natural environment. **Konrad Lorenz (1935)** found that geese seemed to automatically 'attach' to the first thing they see after hatching. This is called **imprinting**.

Imprinting seems to occur during a **'critical period'** — in this example, in the first few hours after birth. After imprinting on something the geese would follow it and use it as a 'role model'. Normally geese would see their mother soon after hatching but Lorenz showed that they could imprint on other things, including him, if they were seen first.

Imprinting is a **fast**, **automatic** process which may be hard to change later. It is unlikely to occur in humans. Our attachments take a **longer** time to develop and we do not automatically attach to particular things — quality care seems more important in human attachment formation (see Schaffer and Emerson, page 12).

...and John Bowlby's Evolutionary Theory...

Bowlby (1951) argued that something like imprinting may occur in humans.
He developed several main claims:

1) We have **evolved** a biological need to attach to our main caregiver — usually our biological mother. This one special attachment is called **monotropy**. Forming this attachment has survival value as staying close to the mother ensures food and protection.

2) This attachment gives us a **'template'** for all future relationships — we learn to trust and care for others. It also acts as a **'safe base'**, giving us confidence to explore our environment.

3) The first 3-5 years of life is the **critical period** for this attachment to develop — otherwise it may never do so.

4) If the attachment doesn't develop or if it is broken, this may seriously damage social and emotional development (see page 16).

Comments on Bowlby's theory:

1) There is some evidence for his claims (see page 16).

2) The claims about monotropy are not supported by Schaffer and Emerson's (1964) findings that many children form multiple attachments, and may not attach to their mother (see page 12).

3) There is mixed evidence for claims of a critical period for attachments to develop (see pages 18-19).

4) Attachments are very important in childhood but the effects of a lack of attachment or having an attachment broken may not be as bad as Bowlby claimed (see pages 16-19).

Practice Questions

Q1   How are the psychodynamic and behaviourist theories of attachment similar?
Q2   Explain how classical and operant conditioning could be involved in forming attachments.
Q3   Why does Harlow's study contradict the psychodynamic and behaviourist theories of attachment?
Q4   What is meant by 'imprinting'?
Q5   Outline Bowlby's claims.
Q6   Why do Schaffer and Emerson's findings contradict Bowlby's claims?

Exam Questions

Q1   Outline one theory of attachment.   [6 marks]

Q2   Explain two criticisms of the theory outlined in question one.   [6 marks]

Monkey lovin'...

As I'm sure you're beginning to realise, psychology is all about theories. You can't get too caught up in them, and you certainly don't need to agree with all of them — but what you have to do is remember the different theories, how they were developed and what the different opinions about them are — only then can you make your own judgements about them.

The Effects of Deprivation and Separation

The attachments we form are very important and there can be serious consequences if they're broken. These pages are all about separation and deprivation, and how they're not the nicest things that can happen to a kid...

Separation and Deprivation are Different in Psychology

Separation is where a child is away from a **caregiver** they're attached to (like their mother). It's about a **relatively short** time, just hours or days, but not a longer or permanent separation.

Deprivation is about the loss of something that is **wanted or needed**. So, 'maternal deprivation' is the loss of the mother (or other attachment figure). A more **long-term** or even **permanent** loss is implied.

Separation Can Have Major Effects

According to several studies, infants or children who have been separated may react through the following stages. The stages are referred to as the **'PDD model'** — Protest, Despair, Detachment:

1) **Protest** During the first few hours, the child will **protest** a lot at being **separated** from its mother (or other attachment figure), by crying, panicking, calling for its mother, etc.

2) **Despair** After a day or two, the child will start to lose interest in its surroundings, becoming more and more **withdrawn**, with occasional crying. They may also eat and sleep less.

3) **Detachment** After a few days, the child will start to become more **alert** and interested again in its surroundings. It will cry less and may seem to have '**recovered**' from its bad reaction to the separation. However, its previous attachment with its carer may now be permanently **damaged** — the trust and security may be lost.

One study to look at...

Robertson and Robertson (1968) — evidence for the PDD model

Method: Several children who experienced short separations from their carers were observed and filmed. For example, a 17 month old boy called John stayed in a residential nursery for nine days while his mother had another baby.

Results: John showed the signs of passing through '**protest**' for the first day or two. Then he showed **despair** — he tried to get attention from the nurses but they were busy with other children so he 'gave up' trying. Then he showed **detachment** — he was more active and content. However, when his mother came to collect him, he was reluctant to be affectionate.

Conclusion: The short-term separation had very **bad effects** on John, including possible **permanent damage** to his attachment with his mother.

Some comments on the PDD model include:

1) These findings suggest that **separating a child from its carers should be avoided** whenever possible. This has important implications for childcare practice, e.g. children should be allowed to visit, or remain with, their mothers during a stay in hospital.

2) The findings of some studies are **open to question**. For example, the effects on John may not have been simply due to separation from his mother — he was also in a strange place and getting much less care and attention than he was used to.

3) **Many factors** influence how a child reacts to a separation. These include age (older children will cope better), the quality of the care received during the separation, the individual temperament of the child and how often it has experienced separations. So, **separations do not necessarily produce the PDD effects**. They may even be good for the child (see pages 20-21).

The Effects of Deprivation and Separation

John Bowlby (1953) Studied Longer Term Maternal Deprivation

Even if short-term separation may not necessarily be bad for a child, **John Bowlby** argued that long-term **deprivation** from an attachment figure could be harmful. He produced his **maternal deprivation hypothesis**:

1) Deprivation from the main carer during the **critical period** (the first 3-5 years), has harmful effects on a child's emotional, social, intellectual and even physical development.

2) Long-term effects of deprivation may include **separation anxiety** (the fear of another separation from the carer). This may lead to problem behaviour, e.g. being very clingy, and avoiding going to school. Future relationships may be affected by this emotional insecurity. Bowlby's research showed evidence for this.

Bowlby (1944) — The 44 Juvenile Thieves

Method:	Case studies were completed on the backgrounds of 44 adolescents who, because of stealing, were referred to the clinic where Bowlby worked.
Results:	It was found that 17 of them had been separated from their mothers for at least six months, some time before five years of age. Some of them didn't seem to care about how their actions affected others. They had no guilty feelings and were called '**affectionless psychopaths**'.
Conclusion:	Deprivation of the child from its main carer early in life can have very **harmful long-term consequences**.

Some comments on Bowlby's maternal deprivation hypothesis include:

1) Other evidence supports Bowlby's claims. **Spitz and Wolf (1946)** found that babies cried more than normal when they were (briefly) maternally deprived. **Goldfarb (1943)** found that orphanage children who were socially and maternally deprived were later less intellectually and socially developed.

2) The evidence has **criticisms**: Bowlby linked the thieves' behaviour to maternal deprivation, but **other things were not considered**, e.g. whether the poverty they grew-up in led them to steal. Spitz and Wolf didn't study **long-term effects**. The children in Goldfarb's study may have been most harmed by the **social deprivation** in the orphanage rather than the maternal deprivation.

Even when deprivation has harmful effects, these may be reversed with appropriate, **quality care**. For example, **Skeels and Dye (1939)** found that children who had been socially deprived (in an orphanage) during their first two years of life quickly improved their IQ scores if they were transferred to a school where they got one-to-one care.

Practice Questions

Q1 Explain the difference between the definitions of separation and deprivation in psychology.
Q2 What is meant by 'PDD'?
Q3 What factors affect how a child reacts to separation?
Q4 Explain Bowlby's maternal deprivation hypothesis.
Q5 Why does the 44 thieves study support Bowlby's hypothesis?
Q6 Give a criticism of the 44 thieves study.

Exam Questions

Q1 Outline the possible effects of maternal separation and maternal deprivation. [6 marks]

Q2 Describe and evaluate Bowlby's maternal deprivation hypothesis. [18 marks]

The PDD model can also be applied as a reaction to excessive study

So, if your mum leaves you alone for a while when you're little you might well become a bank robber — sounds like a pretty poor excuse to me but there you go. It's certainly interesting stuff. Even if you don't agree, the bottom line is you have to learn the theories, who came up with them, and what their pros and cons are — it's a world of pain.

The Effects of Privation

Maternal privation is a bit different to maternal deprivation. **Privation** *means never having been able to satisfy a certain need. So,* **maternal privation** *is when a child has* **never** *had an attachment to their mother or another caregiver. (In contrast to deprivation where an attachment has formed but is broken).*

Privation Means Never Having Been Able to Satisfy a Need

Rutter (1981) claimed that the effects of maternal privation are more likely to be **serious** than the effects of maternal deprivation. Evidence for this comes from **case studies** of children who have suffered difficult conditions or cruel treatment.

Some Case Studies of Privation Include:

Curtiss (1977) — The Case of Genie

This reported the case of a girl who suffered **extreme cruelty** from her parents. Her father believed that she was retarded and kept her strapped to a high chair with a potty in the seat for most of her childhood. She was beaten if she made any sounds, and didn't have the chance to play with toys or with other children or to form an attachment.

She was finally discovered when she was 13 years old. She was **physically under-developed** and could only speak with **animal-like sounds**.

After a lot of help she later learned some language but her **social and intellectual skills never seemed to fully develop**.

Koluchova (1976) — The Case of the Czech twin boys

This is the case of **twin boys** whose mother died soon after they were born. Their father remarried and their stepmother treated them very cruelly. They were often kept locked in a cellar, had no toys and were often beaten.

They were found when they were seven with rickets (a bone development disease caused by a lack of vitamin D), and **very little social or intellectual development**.

They were later adopted and made **much progress**. By adulthood they had above average intelligence and had normal social relationships.

There are a Number of Limitations to this Evidence

1) The children were **not just maternally privated** — they were also privated of general social and intellectual stimulation, and generally treated horribly. So we can't tell what caused the problems.

2) The case studies show **mixed results** for how much children can **recover** from privation early in life. Some recovered well (the Czech twins) but others didn't (Genie).

3) **Differences between the cases** may explain why some recovered better than others did. We should consider:
   a) Length of privation (Genie was the longest).
   b) Experiences during the isolation (the twins may have attached to each other).
   c) Quality of care after the isolation (the twins were adopted, but Genie was passed between psychologists and eventually put in an institution).
   d) Individual differences, including ability to recover (Genie may have been retarded at birth).

The evidence suggests that **recovery from privation is possible**. However, because of the lack of control over what had happened to the children, we can't know for sure exactly what they experienced, e.g. whether they had ever had even a brief attachment. We therefore can't ever be sure why the twins recovered more than Genie.

More controlled, scientific evidence is needed, but it would be ethically very wrong to actually put children in situations of privation to see what might happen. Some studies of children raised in institutions have given some evidence of the effects of privation, but we still can't be precisely sure of the reasons behind the effects seen.

The Effects of Privation

Hodges and Tizard (1989) Studied Children in Institutions

Studies of children raised in **institutions** (e.g. orphanages) may provide **more accurate records** of what the children experienced, seeing as they can be properly scientifically observed over a long period of time. **Hodges and Tizard** studied children in institutions:

Hodges and Tizard (1989) studied children raised in institutions.

Method: This was a longitudinal (long-term) study of 65 children who had been placed in a residential nursery before they were four months old. By four years of age they had each had about 50 different carers, so had been maternally privated. At this time, some returned to their natural mothers, some were adopted and some stayed in the nursery.

Results: At 16 years old, the **adopted** group had **strong** family relationships, although compared to a control group of children from a 'normal' home environment, they had weaker peer relationships. Those who stayed in the **nursery** or who returned to their **mothers** showed **poorer** relationships with family and peers than those who were adopted.

Conclusion: Children can **recover** from early maternal privation if they are in a good **quality**, **loving** environment, although their social development may not be as good as children who have never been privated.

Comment: The sample was quite **small** and more than 20 of the children couldn't be found at the end of the study, so it's hard to generalise the results. However, **Rutter et al (1998)** studied 111 Romanian orphans adopted by British families before they were two years old. The children were initially below normal development, but by four years of age were normal. However, the **older** a child was when they were adopted, the **slower** their development was.

Psychological Research Suggests Two **Long-Term Effects** of Privation

Privation of attachments early in life will have a damaging effect on all aspects of development, although how damaging it will be depends on several factors such as the length of privation. Children can recover to some extent, but **permanent** effects are possible. This can happen in two ways:

1) **Reactive attachment disorder — Parker and Forrest (1993)**
This is a rare but serious condition in which children seem to be permanently damaged by early experiences such as privation of attachment. The symptoms include an inability to give or receive affection, poor social relationships, dishonesty and involvement in crime.

2) **The cycle of privation.** Some evidence (**Quinton et al 1985**), suggests that children who experienced privation may later become less caring parents. Therefore their children are privated of a strong maternal attachment and may then be less caring to their children, and so on.

Practice Questions

Q1 Explain the difference between privation and deprivation.
Q2 What happened to Genie and how well did she recover?
Q3 What happened to the Czech twins and how well did they recover?
Q4 Explain a limitation of case study evidence.
Q5 What does Hodges and Tizard's study show about privation?
Q6 Describe reactive attachment disorder.

Exam Questions

Q1 Explain what is meant by 'separation', 'deprivation' and 'privation'. [6 marks]
Q2 Outline and evaluate research findings on the effects of privation. [15 marks]

Developmental problems — enough to make you develop mental problems

There's some pretty grizzly case studies of seriously abused children on these pages. Not the nicest of topics to be studying, though it is interesting to see how these theories of severe privation fit in with the earlier ones about children separated from their parents and so on. My advice would be get the theories and case studies in your head quickly and move on.

Critical Issue: Day Care and Child Development

*'Day care' refers to any **temporary care** for a child provided by someone other than the parents or relatives they live with. It includes day **nurseries**, **childminders** and **nannies** but does not include residential nurseries or fostering. Psychologists have been interested in whether day care has any positive or negative effects on development.*

There are Concerns That **Day Care** May Affect **Social** Development

It may be necessary for children to have a strong attachment with their main carer before they can learn social skills and form relationships with others (for more information, see pages 16-19).

There has been concern that **day care** may damage social development by disrupting this attachment. However, it could actually help social development by letting children form more friendships and **multiple attachments**.

Several studies have investigated these possibilities:

Belsky and Rovine (1988) — negative effects of day care

Method:	Infants were placed in the '**strange situation**' where different scenarios occurred — a stranger approached, the infant was left alone, the mother returned (see page 13). The strange situation was a test to assess how secure their attachments were. One group had experienced no day care and one had experienced at least 20 hours of day care per week before their first birthday.
Results:	The infants who had received day care were more likely to have an **insecure** attachment type. They were either '**anxious-avoidant**' **(type A)** — ignored their mother and didn't mind if she left, or '**anxious-resistant**' **(type C)** — uneasy around their mother and upset if she left. Those who had not had day care were more likely to be **securely attached** (type B).
Conclusion:	Day care has a **negative** effect on an infant's social development.

Comments:

The results from the 'strange situation' may not be **accurate**. Children who are used to separations may not show distress when their mother leaves because they have developed more **independence**.

However, DiLalla (1998) also found negative effects — the more day care a child had, the **less prosocially** they behaved, i.e. the less they helped, shared, etc.

Shea (1981) — positive effects of day care

Method:	3-4 year-old children were assessed for their social skills during their first 10 weeks of attending a nursery school. One group attended 5 days per week, and the other attended twice a week.
Results:	**Both** groups showed increasing **social skills** (e.g. less aggression and more interaction with others) over the 10 weeks. The group that attended 5 days per week improved more quickly.
Conclusion:	Attending day care has a **positive effect** on social development.

Comments:

This study doesn't tell us whether there were any **long-term effects** on the children. However, Schweinhart et al (1993) found long-term positive effects linked to day care in terms of **less involvement in crime**.

There are Many **Conflicting** Findings on Day Care and Social Development

Many studies show a negative effect, many show a positive effect and some show no effect at all.

It seems that many things influence how day care affects a child, including the child's own **temperament** and the **quality** of the day care that they receive.

For example, **Vandell et al (1988)** found that children who had **good quality** day care were more likely to have **friendly** interactions with others compared to those receiving lower quality day care.

Critical Issue: Day Care and Child Development

There are Also Concerns That **Day Care** May Affect **Cognitive** Development

For intellectual abilities (e.g. reasoning, problem-solving) to develop, a child needs **stimulation** from the environment — playing with toys, exploring new things. They might get this through day care.

However, if a child doesn't have a **secure attachment** as a 'safe base', it may have less confidence to explore. So, day care may have positive or negative effects.

Ruhm et al (2000) — negative effects on cognitive development

Method:	The cognitive abilities of 4000 infants were recorded to compare those who had day care with those who didn't.
Results:	Infants who had day care during their first year showed poorer verbal skills at 3-4 years of age. Having day care at some time during the first three years was also linked to poorer maths and reading skills at 5-6 years of age.
Conclusion:	Day care has **negative effects** on several aspects of cognitive development.

Baydar and Brooks-Gunn (1991) also found that day care during the first year of life had negative effects on cognitive development. However, these results may be due to poor quality day care. Andersson et al (below) studied this.

Andersson et al (1992) — positive effects on cognitive development

Method:	Over 100 Swedish children were followed to investigate the long-term effects of their **high quality** day care. They were assessed for their cognitive and social development using IQ tests and ratings from their teachers.
Results:	Children who began day care before one year of age showed the highest scores at age 8 and 13. Those who never had day care showed the lowest scores.
Conclusion:	High quality day care can have **long-term positive effects** on cognitive development.
Comment:	The children in high quality (therefore expensive) day care may have had **wealthier** families and so also have had a more enriched **home environment**. However, **Project Headstart**, which gave extra day care classes to socially disadvantaged pre-school children, found children in the project later did better in education compared to others. This suggests that positive effects were due to the quality day care rather than the home environment.

There are **Mixed Results** for Day Care's **Effect** on Development

Many things may have an influence on how day care affects development. **Scarr (1998)** identifies several factors — good staff training, adequate space, appropriate toys and activities, having a good ratio of staff to children and trying to minimise staff turnover so children can form stable attachments with carers.

Good quality day care shouldn't have any negative effects and may possibly be beneficial.

Practice Questions

Q1   Describe some evidence showing negative effects of day care on social development.

Q2   What positive effects does Shea's study show?

Q3   Describe some evidence showing positive effects on cognitive development.

Q4   Describe Ruhm et al's findings.

Exam Questions

Q1   Outline research findings on the effects of day care on social development. [6 marks]

Q2   Outline research findings on the effects of day care on cognitive development. [6 marks]

If this is all getting too difficult you can always blame it on your day care...

Let me see if I've got this — if a child is stuck in poor quality day care their social and intellectual skills don't develop so well. If the day care is good and stimulating however, it can have positive effects on the child's development. I don't mean to knock these guys' hard work — but it's not exactly rocket science. Anyway no complaints, it makes it all easier to learn.

Stress as a Bodily Response

I'm sure you all know what stress is. It's having 3 hours left to revise before an exam, or visiting your girlfriend's parents — we all feel it, but this is psychology so it needs a proper scientific explanation.

Stress is a Response to **Stimuli** in the **Environment**

1) Stress can be explained as the **stimulus** in the environment that triggers a stress response. In simpler words, the thing that causes you to act stressed, e.g. a giant cockroach dancing towards you. Psychologists call anything that causes someone to act stressed a '**stressor**'.

2) Stress can also be explained as the **response** to the stimuli — our reaction, e.g. running for the hills.

3) However, the white-coated ones have agreed to explain stress as '**the response that occurs when we think we can't cope with the pressures in our environment**'. This is shown in the diagram below.

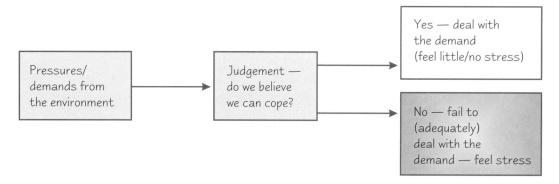

So, stress is the response that occurs when we think the demands being placed on us as are greater than our ability to cope. These are our **own judgements**, so we could over or **underestimate** the demands, or our ability to cope.

Whether the stress is justified or not doesn't matter, if we think we can't cope we get stressed. And when we get stressed something physically changes in us. Hans Selye studied this with stressed-out little rats...

Hans Selye Explained Stress as a **Three Stage Response**

In 1956 Hans Selye was researching the effects of hormones when he noticed that the rats would become ill (e.g. develop stomach ulcers) even when they were given harmless injections.

He concluded that the **stress** of the daily injections **caused the illness** and suggested that all animals and humans react to stressors through a **three stage physiological response**. This is called the **General Adaptation Syndrome (GAS)**.

1) **The Alarm Stage** — when we perceive a stressor our body's first reaction is to increase arousal levels in the body so that we are ready to make any necessary physical response, e.g. if confronted with a big-toothed monster we'd probably run away (the 'fight or flight' response). So our heart rate increases, we breathe more quickly, our muscles tense etc.

2) **The Resistance Stage** — if we are exposed to a stressor for a long time our bodies can adapt to the situation and we seem to be able to cope in a normal way. For example, if we start work in a high pressure situation we would initially be unable to cope and the alarm reaction might frequently occur, but after a while we would seem to adapt. However, even though we might seem to be coping, higher than normal arousal levels would continue in our bodies to deal with the situation.

3) **The Exhaustion Stage** — after long term exposure to a stressor our bodies will eventually be unable to continue to cope with the situation. Alarm signs may return and we may develop illnesses e.g. ulcers, high blood pressure, depression etc. Selye called these 'diseases of adaptation'.

> **Comment** — the stages Selye identified are supported by a lot of scientific research. However, the GAS theory offers a single type of response and so neglects that the body's reaction to stress does vary, e.g. how much adrenaline is released depends on how the stressor is perceived by the person (how frightening etc).
> Also, a certain bacteria has been found to be the cause of ulcers. It could still be the case, though, that stress weakens the immune system making ulcers more likely.

Stress as a Bodily Response

The **Hypothalamus** is the Bit of the Brain that **Responds** to **Stress**

When we perceive a stressor the following chain of events is triggered in the body: (For extra exam marks, learn the full name for these events, which is... wait for it, the **hypothalamic-pituitary-adrenal axis**, wow.)

1) The evaluation of whether something is a stressor occurs in the higher brain centres (the cerebral cortex).

2) When there is a stressor in the environment, these higher areas send a signal to the hypothalamus, which starts two simultaneous processes in the body:

    a) Signals are sent to the **pituitary gland**, which then releases a hormone called **ACTH** (adrenocorticotrophic hormone) into the bloodstream.

       This stimulates the **adrenal cortex** (a structure above the kidneys) to release corticosteroids which help to give us energy by converting fat and protein.

    b) The **Autonomic Nervous System** (ANS) is also activated.

       This stimulates the **adrenal medulla** (a structure close to the adrenal cortex) to release adrenaline and noradrenaline into the bloodstream.

       These lead to an increase in heart rate, blood flow, blood pressure etc.

The result of these changes is that the body is ready to use energy to do whatever action needs to be done, e.g. run away from a dangerous animal.

These **Changes** in the Body Can Be Seen as Having **Survival Value**

1) During our evolution many threats to us would have been from predators or other physical dangers.

2) So, to successfully respond to them would have required energy to fight or run away — the **'fight or flight'** response.

3) However, in **modern society** stressors are more likely to be **psychological** than physical and are more long-term, e.g. the stresses of working at a desk, commuting, noisy neighbours, etc.

4) Therefore the physical stress response is not really needed, but in the long-term it may actually be harmful to our bodies — page 24 explains how.

5) Some stress can be positive and exhilarating — this is known as **eustress**, e.g. a parachute jump might lead to this kind of arousal.

Leo was finding the journey to work increasingly stressful.

Practice Questions

Q1   Outline the different ways of defining stress.

Q2   Describe how Selye discovered the GAS.

Q3   Outline the three stages of the GAS.

Q4   Outline the hypothalamic-pituitary-adrenal axis.

Exam Questions

Q1   Outline the main features of the GAS and give a criticism of it.   [6 marks]

Q2   Describe how the body responds to stress.   [6 marks]

Well, as bodily responses go, I guess stress isn't so bad...

Stress is a natural reaction by your body to anything which threatens you. In the past, it would have been a lion chasing you. Now it's more likely to be a deadline or late train. So next time you see someone getting stressed about something, try telling them, "relax, it could be worse — at least you're not being chased by a lion" — that'll soon calm them down.

Stress and Physical Illness

The last couple of pages made it blindingly obvious that stress isn't just something in your head, it's a physical response. These pages cover what stress can do to your physical state in the long run.

Long-Term Stress Can Affect your Cardiovascular System

The "cardiovascular system" is a fancy name for the **heart** and **blood vessels**.

A **long-term stress response** may have a direct effect on this system:

1) The stored energy (e.g. glucose) that is released during a stressful event is normally re-absorbed by the body after the stressor has gone. But, if the stress is long-term it will **remain** in the blood stream, which may lead to a **blockage**, producing **heart attacks** or **strokes** (if a blood vessel in the brain is blocked).

2) Stress causes a high **heart rate** and **blood pressure**. Over a long time this pressure can **weaken** blood vessels and form **scars** on them.

3) If blood vessels are weakened or damaged, this increases the risk of one **breaking**, which is called a **haemorrhage** (in technical Casualty-speak).

Krantz et al (1991) — stress and the heart

Method:	39 participants did one of three stress-inducing tasks (e.g. a maths test) while the **blood flow** to their hearts and their **blood pressure** were measured.
Results:	The stressful tasks caused **less** bloodflow to the heart (a condition called '**myocardial ischemia**', which is a cause of cardiovascular disorders). The stressful tasks also caused **higher** blood pressure.
Conclusion:	Stress may have a **direct influence** on aspects of body functioning, making cardiovascular disorders more likely.

Comment — Although the effects were clearly linked to stress, it was not shown whether they also occur at other times. They might sometimes happen even if the person feels relaxed and therefore are not simply produced by feeling stressed. Not everybody showed the same reaction, which suggests that differences between the participants may also have a role.

Differences in Personality Might Cause Cardiovascular Problems

Research has shown that as well as stress, certain aspects of personality are linked to cardiovascular disorders.

1) **Friedman and Rosenman (1974)** found that people with a 'type A' personality had an increased risk of heart attack. 'Type A' people are very competitive, always in a hurry and can be very hostile (see page 28 for more detail).

2) **Williams (2000)** also found that feelings of anger are linked to the risk of heart attack:

Williams (2000) — anger and cardiovascular disorders

Method:	A sample of 13,000 participants completed a questionnaire. This asked questions about their feelings of anger — for example, did they ever feel like hitting someone?
Results:	At the beginning of the study, all of the participants were healthy. It was found that those with a **high** score on the anger questionnaire were much more likely to have had a **heart attack** when the sample was checked six years later.
Conclusion:	People who get angry easily / react more angrily have a higher risk of cardiovascular problems.

Comment — Other influences, apart from personality, must also be considered. For example, participants' diet, their occupations, genetic vulnerability, exercise levels, smoking and consumption of alcohol may also influence the development of cardiovascular disorders.

Stress and Physical Illness

Stress Can Also Affect the Immune System

The immune system is made of cells (e.g. white blood cells) and chemicals that **seek and destroy bacteria** and **viruses**. When someone experiences stress over a long time (a **long-term stress response**), their immune system stops functioning properly. Loads of studies have tested whether long-term stress makes us more vulnerable to infection and illness.

Brady et al (1958) — stress and the development of ulcers

Method:	Monkeys were put in pairs and given electric shocks every 20 seconds for 6 hour sessions. One monkey of each pair (the 'executive') could push a lever to delay the shocks. The other could not delay them.
Results:	The 'executive' monkeys were more likely to develop illness (ulcers) and later die.
Conclusion:	The illness and death was not due to the shocks but due to the stress that the executives felt by trying to avoid them. In the long-term, this stress reduced the immune system's ability to fight illness.

Comment — the **ethics** of these methods can be questioned — the experiment was very cruel to the monkeys and would not be allowed today. Also, we cannot generalise results from monkeys to humans. Furthermore, we know that people with little control over their own lives (such as those with low level jobs and the long-term unemployed), experience high levels of stress, which this research cannot explain.

The same Immune System Suppression happens in Humans

Research on humans has also supported the theory that stress can reduce the effectiveness of the immune system, as shown in the following study.

Kiecolt-Glaser et al (1995) — stress and wound healing

Method:	Small samples of skin were taken from 13 women who cared for relatives with Alzheimer's disease. This is a very stressful responsibility. A control group also had samples taken.
Results:	The carers took an average of nine days longer than the controls for the wound to heal.
Conclusion:	Long-term stress impairs the effectiveness of the immune system to heal wounds.

Comment — this is a reliable finding. **Sweeney (1995)** found that people caring for relatives with dementia also took longer than a control group to heal their wounds. However, for both studies the two groups may have varied in other ways apart from the stress of being a carer. The effects on the carers could be due to poor diet, lack of sleep etc, and not just the stress they experienced.

Practice Questions

Q1 Explain what is meant by 'cardiovascular disorder'.
Q2 Outline how stress can lead to cardiovascular disorder.
Q3 How is personality relevant to cardiovascular disorder?
Q4 What is the role of the immune system?

Exam Questions

Q1 Outline the findings of one study of stress and cardiovascular disorder and give a criticism of this study. [6 marks]

Q2 Explain what is meant by the immune system and outline research findings on how it is affected by stress. [6 marks]

Calmer, fitter, happier — more productive...

If you think about it, it kind of stands to reason that being really stressed out all the time will have some effect on your body. You need to remember the actual physiological facts about how this happens and what criticisms all the studies have. Although do take in the lessons for life on these pages — just chill out dude.

Sources of Stress

*There are loads of sources of stress. For some unfortunate individuals it's the thought of peanut butter sticking to their teeth, but for normal folk the two real biggies are **major life changes** and things at **work**.*

Life Changes *are a Source of Stress*

Throughout our lives, we all experience **major life events**, like the death of a close relative, getting married or moving house. These events and the adjustments they cause us to make can be a major source of stress. When psychologists want to find out what level of stress these events cause, they look at health because it's probably linked to stress.

Holmes and Rahe Studied Whether the Stress of Life Changes was Linked to Illness

Approximately 5000 hospital patients' records were studied and any major life events that had occurred before the person became ill were noted. It was found that patients were **likely** to have experienced life changes prior to becoming ill and that **more serious life changes** seemed to be more **linked to stress and illness**. A scale was produced to show the importance of life changes in terms of the stress caused.

...They Ranked Life Events on the Social Re-adjustment Rating Scale (SRRS)

1) **Holmes and Rahe** made a list of 43 common life events and asked loads of people to give a score for each one to say how stressful it was. They called the numbers that made up each score the **Life Change Units (LCU)**. The higher this number of LCUs, the more stressful it was.

2) Then they **ranked** the events from most stressful to least stressful and called it the **Social Re-adjustment Rating Scale (SRRS)**. Examples are shown on the table opposite.

3) And finally, after all that build up, they did a study to see if people who'd experienced more stressful events were more likely to get ill:

Life Event	Rank	Score (LCU)
Death of a spouse	1	100
Divorce	2	73
Retirement	10	45
Death of a friend	17	37
Christmas	42	12

Rahe et al (1970) — LCU score and illness

Method: More than 2500 American Navy seamen were given a form of the SRRS to complete just before they set sail on military duty. They had to indicate all of the events that they had experienced over the previous six months.

Results: Higher LCU scores were found to be linked to a higher incidence of illness over the next seven months. Those who had an LCU score over 150 had a 30% higher risk of illness.

Conclusion: The stress involved in the changes that life events bring is linked to an increased risk of illness.

There are some Issues with the SRRS

1) The link between the **SRRS** and **illness** depends on the accuracy of recall. For example, people might rank recent events higher simply because they can remember them more clearly.

2) The SRRS doesn't separate **positive and negative life events**. Stress and illness might be more linked to negative life changes. For example, a wedding might be stressful, but positive overall, while a funeral might have a very negative stressful effect.

3) Long-term, minor sources of stress, such as everyday **hassles** at work (see page 27), are not considered.

Despite criticisms the SRRS was useful for showing that changes in life may link to stress and illness.

Post-Traumatic Stress Disorder (PTSD) is an example of how major life events can be clearly linked to illness. It is considered to be an **anxiety disorder** and is caused by an extreme life event such as a life-threatening accident. PTSD involves extreme anxiety, difficulties concentrating and sleeping and 'flashbacks' to the event. Some people may need therapy to cope with the disorder, although it's debatable whether therapy does any good.

Sources of Stress

The **Workplace** is a Massive Source of Stress

Most people need to work, but some aspects of the **work they do**, **where they work**, or **who they have to work with**, become a source of stress. This is important because if a person is very stressed at work they may be more likely to get ill. This is not only bad for them, but also for their employer because they will take more days off sick.

Stress in the Workplace comes from **FIVE** Key Areas

1) **Relationships at work** — our relationships with our bosses, colleagues and customers may be stressful, for example if we feel **undervalued** and that we **lack support**.

2) **Work Pressures** — having **too much** work to do, maybe with **strict deadlines**.

3) **The Physical Environment** — where we work may be very noisy, over-crowded or too hot or cold. Also, our work may involve health risks or unsociable working hours.

4) **Stresses linked to our role** — worrying about **job security** or our **prospects for promotion**. Also, the range of our responsibilities may be unclear, and we may experience conflict, e.g. trying to please our bosses and the people who work for us.

5) **Lack of control** — we may not have much **influence over the type and amount of work** we do or where and when we do it. Check out the study by Marmot et al (1997) below:

Marmot et al (1997) — lack of control and illness in the workplace

Method: Over 7000 civil service employees, working in London, were surveyed. Information about their grade of employment, how much control they felt they had, how much support they felt they had etc, was obtained.

Results: When the medical histories of these employees were followed up 5 years later, those on lower employment grades who felt less control over their work (and less social support) were found to be more likely to have cardiovascular disorders.

Conclusion: Believing that you have little control over your work seems to be an important influence on work stress and the development of illness.

Comment — the Marmot lot only looked at 'white collar' work (i.e. office-type jobs), so their results may not apply to other kinds of work. Smoking was also found to be more common in those who developed illnesses. So perhaps those people who felt less control at work were more likely to smoke and the smoking caused the heart problems rather than stress.

Practice Questions

Q1 How did Holmes and Rahe develop their SRRS?
Q2 What did Rahe et al find?
Q3 Explain a criticism of the SRRS.
Q4 What did Marmot et al find?

Exam Questions

Q1 Explain three sources of workplace stress. [6 marks]
Q2 Outline findings of research on life change as a source of stress and give a criticism of this research. [6 marks]

Stress at work — I don't believe it — I live to work...*

As a quick break, make your own SRRS by putting these stressful situations in order: 1) meeting your girl/boyfriend's parents after one shandy too many, 2) watching England in a major qualifying game, it's 0-0 with ten minutes to go, 3) realising that what you are writing will be read by thousands of cynical A-Level students and you're too hungover to write anything funny.

ey made me write this — someone help me get out, I've been typing for weeks without a break... help me...   *SECTION THREE — PHYSIOLOGICAL PSYCHOLOGY*

Stress — Individual Differences

The last few pages have shown how stress affects the body, but that doesn't mean it affects everyone in the same way. If you stick two people in a pit and drop spiders on them, it's unlikely they're going to react in the exact same way. Psychologists call different personal reactions "individual differences".

Different **Personalities** Can Lead to Different Stress Levels

Psychologists love sticking people into groups. One theory about personality is that you can split people into two groups called 'type A' and 'type B'. Type A people are competitive and ambitious. Type Bs are non-competitive, relaxed and easy going. The study below tested how these different types of personality affect the likelihood of CHD (coronary heart disease) — one of the most obvious effects of stress.

Friedman and Rosenman (1974) — 'type A' personality and illness

Method: Approximately 3000, 39-59 year old American males were assessed for their personality characteristics, using interviews and observation.

Results: Eight years later, 257 of them had developed **CHD** (coronary heart disease). 70% of these were classed as 'type A' personality. This includes being 'workaholic', extremely competitive, hostile to others, concerned with time and always in a rush. Type B is the opposite, being less competitive, less impatient and less hostile.

Conclusion: Type A personalities seem to be at a **higher risk** of CHD.

Comments —

1) Only two personality types seems a bit simplistic. Later research also identified **Type C** personalities — mild-mannered, easy-going people who may not react well to stressful situations and suppress their emotions. These people seem to have a higher risk of **cancer**. **Type D** personalities were identified as very negative/pessimistic people who worry too much about things and lack social skills. These people seem more at risk from **heart attacks**.

2) This research doesn't prove that personality characteristics can **cause** stress and illness. It could be the other way round. For example, Type A personality may develop as a **response** to being under stress (from work etc). Also, the samples used in studies have been quite limited — mostly white, middle-class, middle-aged, male Americans.

Stress can be Related to **Culture**

Culture is a really vague term that is used to group people by **beliefs**, **behaviours**, **morals** or **customs** they share. Culture has a big impact on how people live and how others react to them. So those white-coated people have done different studies to find out how a person's culture affects their level of stress.

Biological Studies — Cooper et al (1999) suggested that the higher level of cardiovascular disorder that is found in African-Americans could be due to genes, more commonly found in this group, which may contribute to higher blood-pressure. However, they also found that high blood pressure was more likely in Africans who lived in more urbanised countries (like America) than those who live in more rural countries (like Nigeria). This suggests a **social influence**.

Social Studies — higher stress and blood pressure might be found in people in urban areas because of factors like overcrowding, pollution and high unemployment. However, **Adams-Campbell et al (1993)** found that African-American women had higher blood pressure than white women who were of the same **social-economic group** (i.e. people who have the same lifestyle and money).

Cognitive Studies — African-Americans may experience more prejudice which may lead to more negative thoughts and beliefs ('cognitions'). They encounter more difficulties and threats in society which may lead to more stress and so more illness.

Comment — biological, social and cognitive factors influence the links between culture, stress and illness. It is difficult to identify the exact influence of each of them because we cannot do controlled experiments involving genetics or prejudice due to ethical issues. It is also more likely that cardiovascular disorder is due to a number of factors in combination rather than just one single factor.

Stress — Individual Differences

Stress can also be Related to *Gender*

Men and woman are pretty different in lots of ways, so psychologists (who don't miss a trick) thought that maybe these differences could affect what kinds of thing men and women find stressful and how they cope. They looked at how biological, social and cognitive differences between males and females influence their response to stress.

Biological Explanation — males and females may have **evolved** different physiological responses to stress due to their roles during the early evolution of humans. To be better adapted at their roles of 'hunter-gatherers', males might have evolved a stronger 'fight or flight' response than women, who had the roles of child-carers.

Taylor et al (2000) claim that women's hormones produce a calmer response to stress and make it more likely that they seek social support to help them cope. However, it can be argued that social factors may explain gender differences in coping methods.

Social Explanation — all cultures have developed **stereotyped social roles** for men and women, relating to what beliefs, behaviours and occupations they 'should' have. A western stereotype has been that men are (or should be) less open about their feelings. So, they may be less open about feeling stressed and more likely to use **harmful coping methods** like drinking and smoking.

Carroll (1992) found that women do generally make more use of social support to deal with stress. This healthier way of coping may explain why women have a lower risk of **CHD** (coronary heart disease). However, Carroll (1992) also found there has been an increase in rates of CHD in women. This could relate to changing stereotypes, as more women now also drink and smoke.

Cognitive Explanation — males and females may differ in how they interpret stressful situations and think about ways of reacting. For example, **Vogele et al (1997)** claim that women are better able to control anger and therefore respond more calmly to stressful situations. Men may feel that anger is an acceptable way to respond, and feel stress if they cannot show it. These cognitive differences could be the result of biology **or** the roles we are taught to follow or a bit of both.

Comment — it's dangerous to make sweeping generalisations about **all** men and women responding to stress in particular ways. Someone's response to stress will also be affected by other stuff, like their culture, their personality and their individual coping methods.

Practice Questions

Q1 Explain the differences between personality types A, B, C and D.
Q2 Give a criticism of Friedman and Rosenman's research.
Q3 How are biological, social and cognitive factors relevant to understanding culture differences in stress?
Q4 How are biological, social and cognitive factors relevant to understanding gender differences in stress?

Exam Questions

Q1 Describe one study of stress and personality. [6 marks]

Q2 Consider how culture and/or personality are linked to stress. [18 marks]

We are all individuals, we are all individuals, we are all individuals...

This is an important thing to remember throughout psychology. People are divided into groups to show how different things affect people — but there are also individual differences, which means that when put in the same situation, people will often react differently. This seems pretty obvious but it's easy to forget if you get too wrapped up in all the theories.

Critical Issue: Stress Management

Finally, we've got to a bit where psychologists are trying to actually help people rather than just prodding them. There are two main types of treatment — physiological and psychological methods. And here they are...

Physiological Methods of Stress Management use Drugs and Biofeedback

Both drug therapy and biofeedback help people cope with **stress** by changing the way their body **responds** to it.

1) Drug therapy — the drugs used work in two ways

1) They **slow down** the activity of the **central nervous system** (CNS).

Anti-anxiety drugs called **benzodiazepines** (BZs) help the body react to its own natural anxiety-relieving chemical **GABA** (gamma-amino-butyric acid), which slows down the activity of neurones and makes us feel relaxed.

2) They **reduce** the activity of the **sympathetic nervous system** (SNS).

The SNS increases heart rate, blood pressure and levels of the hormone **cortisol**. High levels of cortisol can make our immune system **weak** and also cause heart disease. The group of drugs called **beta-blockers** reduce all these unpleasant symptoms.

2) Biofeedback — the person learns to relax

Biofeedback — The person **learns** how to control and **regulate** the symptoms of stress so that they feel **relaxed** in real-life stressful situations. There are 4 steps involved:

1) The person is attached to a machine that monitors and gives **feedback** on heart rate or blood pressure.

2) The person learns to **control** the symptoms of stress by taking deep breaths which slow down their heart rate. This makes them feel relaxed.

3) Relaxation acts like a **reward** and encourages the person to repeat this as an involuntary activity.

4) The person learns to use this in **real-life** situations.

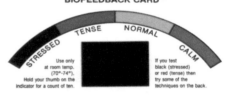

An attempt at making biofeedback a more accessible therapy.

The Physiological Approach Has Strengths and Weaknesses

Both drugs and biofeedback are effective:

Drugs are **quick** and **effective** in reducing dangerous symptoms such as high blood pressure. **Kahn et al (1986)** found that BZs were superior to a placebo (sugar pill) when they tracked 250 patients over an 8-week period.

Attanasio et al (1985) found that biofeedback helped teenagers and children with stress related disorders to gain **control** over the symptoms of **migraine** headaches. They also showed an increase in **enthusiasm** and a more positive attitude.

BUT both treat symptoms rather than the underlying causes of stress:

Drugs only help with the **symptoms** and only so long as the drugs are taken.

Biofeedback also aims to **reduce** symptoms, but using relaxation techniques can also give the person a sense of **control** and have more long lasting benefits.

Placebos are pills that do nothing at all. They're used to test if any effect happens just because people <u>think</u> they're being treated.

Drugs have side effects, biofeedback doesn't:

Drugs can have minor **side effects** such as dizziness and tiredness or more serious effects such as blurred vision and changes in sex drive. **Withdrawal symptoms** such as increased anxiety, seizures, tremors and headaches when people come off medication can be distressing. BZs can be **addictive**, and are generally limited to a maximum of 4 weeks' use.

There are no side effects of biofeedback, just **relaxation**. This method's advantage is that it is **voluntary** and not invasive.

Drugs are easier to use than biofeedback:

Drugs are relatively **easy** to prescribe and use.

Biofeedback needs specialist **equipment** and expert **supervision**. Some argue the benefits of biofeedback could be gained from other relaxation techniques and so this is an unnecessary expense.

Critical Issue: Stress Management

Psychological Methods Are About Learning to Think Differently

The psychological approach helps the person to cope better by **thinking differently** about the stressful situation. These techniques have been shown to be **effective** and deal with the **source** of the problem rather than just the symptoms. They provide **skills** that have more lasting value — like the **confidence** to cope with future problems and the belief of being in **control** and seeing life as a challenge rather than as a threat. (And other cheesy, upbeat things like that).

Meichenbaum's Stress Inoculation Technique (SIT):

This works like immunisation. Just like you might be inoculated against any attack from disease, you can protect yourself from the harmful effects of stress. **Training** involves preparation so that you can deal with stress before it becomes a problem.
3 steps are involved:

1) **Conceptualisation:** Identify fears and concerns with therapist's help.

2) **Skill acquisition and rehearsal:** Train to develop skills like positive thinking and relaxation in order to improve self confidence.

3) **Application and follow-through:** Practice newly acquired skill in real life situations with support and back up from therapist.

Meichenbaum (1977) found that SIT works both with short-term stressors such as preparing for public speaking, and longer-term stressors such as medical illness, divorce or work related stress.

Hardiness Training:

Kobasa suggests that a strong and hardy person shows **3 Cs**: **Control** over their lives, **commitment** (a sense of purpose in life) and **challenge** (life is seen as a challenge and opportunity rather than as a threat).

Maddi introduced a training programme to increase hardiness, arguing that the more hardy the person, the better they cope with stress. This training has 3 steps:

1) **Focusing:** Learn to **recognise** physical symptoms of stress, e.g. increase in heart rate, muscle tension and sweating.

2) **Reliving stressful encounters:** Learn to analyse stressful situations to better understand possible coping strategies.

3) **Self improvement:** Take on **challenges** that can be coped with and build **confidence**, thereby gaining a greater sense of **control**.

Maddi (1998) got 54 managers who went on a hardiness training programme to report back on their progress. They recorded an increase in hardiness and job satisfaction and decrease in strain and illness.

Despite proven effectiveness, there are **weaknesses** with psychological methods:

1) Psychological methods only suit a narrow band of very **determined** individuals.
2) Research is based on white middle class business folk and so can't necessarily be **generalised** to others.
3) The procedures are very lengthy and require considerable **commitment** of time and effort.
4) The **concepts** may be too complex. For example, a lack of hardiness may be just another label for negativity. It might be argued that it is just as effective to relax and think positively.

Practice Questions

Q1 Describe two ways in which drug therapy helps in stress management.
Q2 What are the four steps involved in biofeedback?
Q3 In what way is biofeedback better than drug therapy?
Q4 What does SIT stand for and what three stages does it involve?

Exam Questions

Q1 Describe and evaluate one physiological approach used in managing the negative effects of stress. [6 marks]

Q2 Give one strength and one weakness of the psychological approach to stress management. [6 marks]

Stress management — quite the opposite of traditional management...

This ridiculously stressed and hectic lifestyle we choose to live is turning us all into ill people. I can't understand it myself — personally I choose the more Caribbean attitude to time management. I'm quite confident I'll never need to take BZs or teach myself to think differently. But then again, I might get into trouble for not finishing this book on time. Hmmm...

The Role of Control in Stress

Things are a lot less scary if you're in control — stress isn't any different. You often can't control what causes the stress, but you can control how it affects you. It's all about how you view stress and what you do to cope.

How We **View** Stress is More Important Than Stress Itself

The **transactional model of stress** suggests that people differ in how they **view** a stressful situation. For example, one person being made redundant at work might feel **devastated**, while another might feel **positive** about the opportunities it opens up.

Lazarus (1966) believed that our **perception** of the 'stressor' (the source of stress) is more important than the stressor itself. If we feel we have some **control** in dealing with the demands of a stressful situation, then we are more likely to cope with it than if we feel we have no control over it.

Control over How we View Stressors Affects How Stressed we Get

There are 6 studies to learn about how a **lack of control** can either cause or enhance stress:

Perceived locus of control means who or what people think is in control of their lives.

① **Seligman (1974)** conducted a study where two groups of dogs were given electric shocks. One group could press a lever to stop the shock, the other group couldn't. Both groups received the same amount of shocks, but when later given the chance to escape, the dogs with no previous control didn't even try. This is known as **learned helplessness**. Seligman believed that human **depression** can also be explained in terms of learned helplessness.

② **Rotter (1966)** believed that the perceived **locus of control** affects how stressed people get. People can be described as one of two types:

Externalisers — They believe good things happen due to luck and bad things are someone else's fault. Such people are more likely to become **anxious** as they perceive no sense of control over anything.

Internalisers — This type of person takes **personal responsibility** for both good and bad events in life. Such individuals are more likely to feel a sense of control and therefore take steps to **cope** with stress.

③ **Suls and Mullen (1981)** found that illness was associated more with **uncontrollable** life events than with **controllable** life events.

④ **Marmot (1997)** found that people in jobs with less responsibility showed higher risk of **cardiovascular disease**. These people reported low job **control**, poor social support and no control over decision making processes at work.

This study used a potentially biased sample — urban civil servants who may be quite job-oriented and ambitious. Additionally, the results could be explained by socio-economic status (SES). People of low SES are statistically more likely to smoke, live in stressful environments and have poor diets — factors which are also related to cardiovascular disease.

⑤ However, **Schaubroeck (2001)** found that employees who believed that they were responsible for things going wrong at work were more stressed (no shock, Sherlock). This suggests that greater control isn't always better for some people or for some situations.

⑥

Glass and Singer (1972) investigated the illusion of control.

Aim:	To investigate whether the **illusion** of control can reduce stress. The 'illusion of control' means that people think they're in control, but they aren't really.
Method:	Participants in the experimental group were deceived into believing that they could **control** a loud noise by pressing a button. Their stress response was compared with a control group of participants who were simply exposed to the loud noise. Their arousal level was measured using the **galvanic skin response** (GSR). GSR is simply a measure of increased sweating, and hence increased electrical conductivity, which indicates increased stress.
Results:	The experimental group showed **less** stress response (lower arousal level) compared to the control group.
Conclusion:	If people think they are in control (even when they're not), they are less likely to get stressed.

The Role of Control in Stress

Informational *and* Cognitive *Control Are Useful Together*

Informational control is having some **knowledge** on the nature of the stress so that a person can plan to cope with it.
Cognitive control is control over stress through **relaxation** to avoid negative thinking and increase positive thinking.
Langer et al investigated the effectiveness of these two methods of control:

Langer et al (1975) studied the types of control.

Aim:	To compare three groups of patients who were undergoing non-emergency surgeries, investigating the **effectiveness** of **informational** and **cognitive control**.
Method:	One group was given informational control — they were **informed** about the nature of the treatment and the effect this would have on them in the days to follow. The second group was given cognitive control — they were prepared to **think** positively and avoid negative thoughts about the surgery. A third group was not prepared in any specific way. This served as the **comparison** group.
Results:	The first two groups coped far **better** than the comparison group.
Conclusion:	Both informational and cognitive control increase people's ability to cope with stress. For maximum benefit, there is no reason why they shouldn't be used **together**.

Stress Management *Techniques Use Cognitive Control*

Stress management techniques aim to **increase cognitive control** and minimise the negative effects of stress.
A simple method is to say things to yourself that will help you cope with stressful situations:

Self instructions that can help us to cope better		
Preparation	**Confronting the situation**	**Reinforcing self statement**
What is the point in worrying?	Take a deep breath.	That worked.
It is not the end of the world.	I can only do one thing at a time.	It was not so bad after all.
What is the worst that could happen?	I will focus on this task for now.	I always knew I could do it.

Practice Questions

Q1 Describe the theory of learned helplessness.

Q2 Why does Rotter think externalisers are less able to cope with stress?

Q3 What did Marmot discover about the link between workplace conditions and stress?

Q4 Name two types of control that are helpful in managing stress.

Exam Questions

Q1 Outline the procedure and findings of any one study on the role of control in stress. [6 marks]

Q2 Describe the findings of research on the role of control in stress. [6 marks]

Aaaaaaaaaaaaaaaaaaaaaaaaaaaarrrrrrrrrrrrrrrrrrrrrrrggggggggggggghhhhhhhh...

Makes sense doesn't it? You get bossed around, told to write huge essays, told to write them again, told you can't go out until you've done your essay — of course you're going to feel stressed, it's only natural. But if you insist to yourself that it's all your own choice because it's the only path to a good job and lots of money, then you'll feel better. In theory anyway...

Defining Abnormality

Defining what's abnormal is easy — it's just what's not normal — but what's normal...?

Some Behaviours are **Rare** Within a Population

The concept of deviation from the majority is expressed in terms of **normal distribution**:

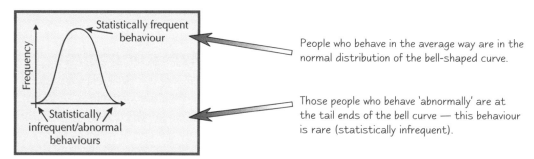

People who behave in the average way are in the normal distribution of the bell-shaped curve.

Those people who behave 'abnormally' are at the tail ends of the bell curve — this behaviour is rare (statistically infrequent).

However there are **problems** with defining abnormality simply in terms of statistical infrequency —

1) It doesn't take account of the **desirability of behaviour**, just its frequency. For example, a very high IQ is abnormal, as is a very low one, but the high IQ is desirable and the low IQ is undesirable.

2) There is **no distinction** between **rare, slightly odd** behaviour and **rare, psychologically abnormal** behaviour.

3) There is **no definite cut-off point** of where normal behaviour becomes abnormal behaviour.

4) Some behaviours are psychologically abnormal, but quite common, e.g. mild depression. **Hasset and White (1989)** argue that you cannot use statistical infrequency to define abnormality because of this. Using the statistical infrequency idea, some disorders would not be classed as anything unusual.

Interestingly, as recently as the 80s, homosexuality was considered a **clinical syndrome**. It was described as a **sexual deviation** and was only dropped from the American Psychiatric Association's Diagnostic and Statistical Manual (DSM) in 1987. The diagnosis was dropped because it was found that homosexuality was **not as infrequent** as previously thought and that homosexuals did not differ from heterosexuals in terms of **psychological wellbeing**.

Abnormality Can Also be Described as **Deviation From Social Norms**

1) All societies have their **standards** of behaviour and attitudes. Deviating from these can be seen as abnormal. This can also be described as 'departing from the expected'.

2) But **cultures vary**, so there isn't one universal set of social 'rules'.

3) The problem with defining abnormality as deviation from social norms is that it can be used to justify the removal of some people from a society. For example, people opposing a particular political regime could be said to be abnormal.

Malinowski provided an example of how behaviours that would be considered abnormal in our western culture, can be considered perfectly normal and functional in others:

Malinowski observed the hunter-gatherer Trobriand islanders.

1) He observed how they satisfied their **basic needs** (food, shelter), their **derived needs** (defence, social control) and their **integrative needs** (psychological security, social harmony etc.).

2) He found that the islanders used **magic** and **ritual** before embarking on dangerous deep sea fishing, but not before safe lagoon fishing.

3) He viewed this superstition or magic as perfectly **rational**.

4) He thought that the magic functioned to **reduce anxiety** and tension associated with the dangers of deep sea fishing.

5) In modern western society, the use of magic in this way would possibly be considered '**abnormal**'. In the culture of the Trobriand islands, however, Malinowski did not consider it unusual, but as serving a need for the islanders. In western society, praying might be seen as serving a similar purpose.

Defining Abnormality

Jahoda (1958) Identified Six Conditions Associated With Good Mental Health

Jahoda's six conditions were:
1) Positive self attitude
2) Self-actualisation (realising your potential, being fulfilled)
3) Resistance to stress
4) Personal autonomy (making your own decisions, being in control)
5) Accurate perception of reality
6) Adaptation to the environment

However, it would be **hard to meet** all the standards set in this list, and they are **subjective** (ideas of what is required for each will differ from person to person).

Also, a violent offender, for example, may have a positive self attitude and be resistant to stress etc, yet society would not consider them to be in good mental health.

The Idea of Ideal Mental Health Varies Across Time and Between Cultures

What is considered mentally 'healthy' at one time, would not be at another.
For example, in some cultures today, it is considered **abnormal** for women to **enjoy sex** and they may be forced to have their clitoris surgically removed to prevent their enjoyment. In Victorian times here, women who enjoyed sex were deemed abnormal and hence Freud coined the term '**nymphomania**'. There is still influence from this and so today there are still **double standards** about male and female sexual activity.

But the idea of 'ideal' mental health can be a useful one because it moves away from focusing on mental 'illness'.

Some Symptoms are Associated With Mental Illness

The Department of Health provides a guide to assess symptoms associated with mental illness.
To be classified as a mental illness, there should be **one or more** of the following (**not temporary**) symptoms:

1) Impairment of **intellectual functions** that is not temporary, such as memory and comprehension.
2) Alterations to **mood** that lead to **delusional appraisals** of the past or future, or lack of any appraisal.
3) Delusional **beliefs**, such as persecution or jealousy.
4) Disordered **thinking** — the person may be unable to appraise their situation or communicate with others.

Practice Questions

Q1   What is the statistical infrequency definition of abnormality?
Q2   What does Jahoda (1958) say are the six conditions associated with mental health?
Q3   Define abnormality using the deviation from social norms explanation.
Q4   Describe Malinowski's findings.

Exam Questions

Q1   Discuss the idea of mental health in relation to different cultures.   [6 marks]

Q2   Compare the deviation from social norms definition and the statistical infrequency definition of abnormality. [6 marks]

I'm not abnormal — I'm just a little statistically infrequent

The fact that homosexuality was, until very recently, classed as a sexual deviation and a form of abnormality goes to show just how difficult defining normal and abnormal is. It varies with culture and time and is very difficult to define in any scientific way. What's important is that you understand why and how people have attempted to define it.

Defining Abnormality

I'm beginning to think it's just wrong to try and define abnormality. I mean, for starters, calling someone 'abnormal' just isn't very nice. More to the point, it seems almost impossible to define.

The Concept of Abnormality **Varies** From One Culture and Time to Another

1) **Cultural relativism** means that judgements we make in relation to abnormality are relative to individual cultures. That's because what's normal in one culture is sometimes abnormal in another. So definitions of abnormality are **limited** because they're **culturally specific**.

2) It's important to work out whether the abnormality is **absolute**, **universal**, or **culturally relative**.

> a) **Absolute** — occurring in the same way and frequency across cultures.
>
> b) **Universal** — present in all cultures, but not with the same frequency.
>
> c) **Culturally relative** — unique to that particular culture.

3) Many **physical** conditions are **absolute**, as are some mental conditions e.g. **schizophrenia**. However, **social norms** vary from one culture to another. This can affect how these conditions are **perceived**. For example, in some countries such as Puerto Rica it is considered **normal** to experience hallucinations, but in the western world it can be seen as a symptom of schizophrenia.

4) Some abnormal behaviours are **universal**, e.g. **depression** occurs in all cultures, but is more common in women and in industrial societies.

5) Some abnormal behaviours are **culturally relative** — these are known as **culture-bound syndromes**.

> '**Witiko**' is an example of culturally relative behaviour. It is a culture-bound syndrome, suffered by native Canadians, who **lose their appetite** for ordinary food, feel **depressed** and believe they are **possessed by the Witiko**, who is a **giant man-eating monster**. This can result in cannibalism, murder or pleas for death from the sufferer. It is thought to be an extreme form of **starvation anxiety**.

Attempts to **Define** Abnormality May Be **Biased**

There are often problems when it comes to defining abnormality — these often relate to **stereotypes**.

> ### Gender...
>
> Factors such as **biological** or hormonal differences, and the different ways that men and women are **brought up**, could lead to gender differences in the frequencies of disorders.
>
> However, the **gender stereotype** can lead people to believe that women are generally moodier, and men generally more violent and anti-social. This could be a factor in clinicians tending to diagnose more **mood** disorders in women and more **anti-social** disorders in men — the clinicians expect to find them.

> ### Race...
>
> Several studies have found that very large numbers of **black people** in Britain are being diagnosed with **schizophrenia**. Surveys of inpatients by **Bagley (1971)** and **Cochrane (1977)** found that immigrant groups in Britain are more likely to be diagnosed as schizophrenic than native-born people. This is particularly so for people originating in Africa, the Caribbean and Asia. It was thought at first that this could be explained in terms of genetic or biological factors, except that the same rates of occurrence were not found in the countries of origin.
>
> Therefore, possible reasons include **racial stereotypes** in diagnosis and **greater stress**. Stress could be due to poorer living conditions, prejudice, or the general stress of living in a new culture.

Even if stereotypes alone are to blame for a diagnosis, the person could 'develop' the disorder: Once a person is **labelled** with a mental disorder, they may begin to behave in the expected way due to the label. The diagnosis then becomes a **self-fulfilling prophecy**.

Defining Abnormality

Classification Systems **Pigeon-hole** People

A major **problem** with classification systems of abnormality is that they can lead to pigeon-holing people into **certain categories**. This leads to **practical**, **theoretical** and **ethical considerations**, which **you need to know**.

1) **Diagnosis** — When people report how they feel 'psychologically', these are subjective feelings. One person's "I'm extremely depressed" may mean the same as someone else's, 'I'm fed up'. A more **idiographic approach** would be useful — that is, focusing on each unique case and viewing patients on their merits.

2) There are many **different theories** — psychodynamic, learning, cognitive theory etc. They all have their own definitions and ideas on what causes abnormality.

3) There is little evidence of **validity** — how much the classification system measures what it's supposed to. It is hard to find a central cause (**aetiology**) for most disorders. If patients have more than one disorder it can be difficult to spot symptoms of one disorder.

4) Psychiatrists may not always agree from category to category, so classification systems may not always be **reliable**.

5) **Treatment** — Grouping patients can help to find treatments, but treatment often depends on diagnosis. Therefore, if the diagnosis is subjective initially, treatment may not be correct.

6) **Labelling theory (Scheff, 1966)** argues that if people are treated as mentally ill, their behaviour will change and become more like that expected from their diagnosis.

7) **Szasz (1974)** said that psychiatric labels were **meaningless**. He said illness was a bodily problem, so 'mental' illness could not exist. He believed the term was used to exclude non-conformists from society.

8) Finally, it is hard to say where normality ends and abnormality starts anyway.

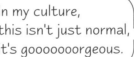

In my culture, this isn't just normal, it's gooooooorgeous.

Practice Questions

Q1 What is cultural relativism?

Q2 What are culture-bound syndromes?

Q3 Give an example of a culture-bound syndrome.

Q4 Briefly define labelling theory.

Q5 What is an idiographic approach to abnormality?

Exam Questions

Q1 Discuss the concept of cultural relativism in relation to abnormality. [6 marks]

Q2 Discuss the drawbacks of the use of classification systems for defining abnormality. [6 marks]

In the seventies people even thought men with huge perms were normal...

You've got to know all the stuff on these pages if you're going to answer a "defining abnormality" question in the exam. I reckon the best way is to read the pages and make a list of all the main points in note form. Then cover the pages up, and just try to write them out again from the notes you've just made. I know it's tough and dull, but it'll help you learn.

The Biological Model of Abnormality

There are many different models of abnormality that describe symptoms and treatments differently.
You need to know the biological model's explanations of causes and treatments, and its strengths and weaknesses.

The Biological Model Assumes Psychological Disorders are **Physical Illnesses**

The **biological (or medical or somatic) model** assumes that psychological disorders are **physical illnesses** with physical causes, in principle no different from physical illnesses like flu, except they have major psychological symptoms.

When the same symptoms frequently occur together, they represent a reliable **syndrome** or **disorder**.
The cause or 'aetiology' may be one or more of the following:

1) **Genetics** — Faulty genes are known to cause some diseases that have psychological effects e.g. Huntington's disease that leads to a deterioration of mental abilities.

2) **Neurotransmitters** — These are chemicals that allow brain cells to send signals to each other. Too much or too little of a particular neurotransmitter may produce psychological disorders, e.g. an increased level of **dopamine** is linked to schizophrenia — **drugs** like cocaine, which increase dopamine levels, can lead to schizophrenia-like symptoms.

3) **Infection** — Disorders may be caused by infection. **General paresis** is a condition involving delusions and mood swings, leading to paralysis and death. It is caused by **syphilis**, and can now be treated.

4) **Brain injury** — Accidental brain damage may produce psychological disorders. For example, **Phineas Gage** was involved in building a railway line in 1800s America. Dynamite accidentally exploded, sending an iron rod through his head, destroying parts of his frontal lobes. He miraculously survived, but he became more impulsive, disorganised, couldn't plan for the future and had a strangely different personality.

Biological Disorders Can Be **Treated** With Biological Therapies

The biological model says that once the physical cause of a psychological disorder has been identified, a physical (biological) therapy is needed to treat the physical problem. One or more of the following may be used:

1) **Drugs** — Drugs can be used to change **neurotransmitter levels** in the brain. For example, **phenothiazines** reduce levels of dopamine and can therefore relieve symptoms of schizophrenia.

2) **Psychosurgery** — Psychosurgery is brain surgery involving destruction or separation of parts of the brain. **Moniz** developed the '**frontal lobotomy**' in the 1930s to separate the frontal lobes from the rest of the brain. This reduced aggression and generally made people more placid. However, it is **not a cure**, it's a change — the **irreversible** changes to personality may have just made patients easier to manage. Psychosurgery is now only a last resort treatment for some disorders, e.g. very serious depression.

3) **Electro-convulsive therapy (ECT)** — ECT is an electric shock of about 100-150 volts given to a person's brain. This can help relieve depression, but can also produce memory loss. Although quite commonly used in the past, it's now only a last resort therapy.

The **Biological Model** Has **Strengths** and **Weaknesses**

Strengths:

a) It has a **scientific** basis in biology and a lot of evidence shows that biological causes **can** produce psychological symptoms.

b) It can be seen as **ethical** because people are **not to blame** for their disorders. They just have an illness.

c) Biological **therapies** have helped relieve conditions (e.g. schizophrenia) that could not be treated previously.

Weaknesses:

a) Biological therapies raise **ethical** concerns. Drugs can produce addiction and may only suppress symptoms, not cure the disorder. The effects of psychosurgery are irreversible.

b) Psychological disorders may not be linked to any physical problem and **psychological therapies** can be just as effective as biological treatments, without any interference to biological structures.

The Psychodynamic Model of Abnormality

The Psychodynamic Model is Based On Conflict in Development

1) According to the **psychodynamic model**, abnormality is the result of problems in childhood.

2) The model is based on **Freud's** division of personality into the id, ego and superego.

3) It also uses his stages of development — the oral, anal, phallic, latency and genital stages.

4) The model suggests that conflict and anxiety may occur during childhood because the **ego** is not yet **developed** enough to deal with the id's desires, understand real-world issues or cope with the super-ego's moral demands.

5) Psychological disorders may also come from **conflict** or anxiety which happens in a certain stage of development. For example, during the anal stage, conflict may occur during potty training.

6) Anxiety from the conflicts is repressed into the **unconscious mind**.

7) **Stress** or **trauma** in adulthood may 'trigger' the repressed conflicts, leading to **psychological disorders**.

The Psychodynamic Model Also Has Strengths and Weaknesses

Strengths:

1) It's quite a unique approach to abnormality, suggesting that childhood experiences are important and that disorders may be linked to unresolved conflicts related to biological needs.

2) It offers a method of therapy. **Psychoanalysis** uses **dream analysis** to reveal unconscious desires. They also use '**free association**', to analyse what the person freely says. This may also uncover unconscious conflicts. The client can then understand the causes of their problems and so resolve them and release their anxieties.

Weaknesses:

1) Freud's claims are based on his subjective interpretations of his patients' dreams etc. Therefore they are hard to **scientifically test** and so cannot be proven right or wrong.

2) **Psychoanalysis** may take a long time and so be very expensive. The childhood conflicts that are 'uncovered' may be emotionally distressing and possibly inaccurate, depending on the reliability of the patient's memory and the analyst's interpretations.

Practice Questions

Q1 What causes psychological disorders according to the biological model?

Q2 What methods of therapy are used in the biological model?

Q3 Provide a strength and a weakness of the biological model.

Q4 Why are the id, ego and super-ego in conflict with each other?

Q5 Explain the methods used in psychoanalysis.

Exam Questions

Q1 Outline the assumptions of the biological model in terms of the causes of abnormality. [6 marks]

Q2 Outline the assumptions of the psychodynamic model in terms of the treatment of abnormality. [6 marks]

So it's either electric shocks, or chatting about your childhood...

These are very different approaches to dealing with abnormality — the biological model suggests psychological illness is much the same as any other illness and can be treated with medicine. The psychodynamic model, by contrast, concentrates on vague psychological effects of events in your childhood — now that's as different as chalk and cheese.

The Behavioural Model of Abnormality

Bet you thought you'd finished with the models of abnormality... Never — not without behavioural and cognitive models...

The Behavioural Model of Abnormality says **Behaviours** are all **Learnt**

Behaviourists argue that abnormal behaviours are learnt in the same way that all behaviours are learnt — through classical and operant conditioning. This page is all about their take on the matter.

1) Behaviourists reckon that classical conditioning can be used to explain the development of many abnormal behaviours, including **phobias** and **taste aversions**. In classical conditioning, a certain stimulus (**unconditioned stimulus** or **UCS**) triggers a natural reflex (**unconditioned response** or **UCR**). When some other stimulus (**conditioned stimulus** or **CS**) is repeatedly presented with the UCS, over time it will elicit the UCR by itself. The response is then called the **conditioned response**, or **CR**.

Phobias can be created when the natural fear response is associated with a particular stimulus.

Watson and Rayner (1920) experimented with an 11 month old boy, **'Little Albert'**, producing fear of a white rat by associating it with a loud, scary noise.

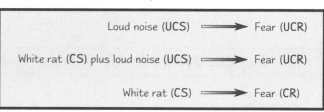

Taste aversions are often created if a person is ill after a certain food or drink. Its taste will become a CS, producing a CR of nausea. So, if you were ill after eating a curry with bad meat, the taste of curry might always make you feel ill.

2) **Operant conditioning** — Operant conditioning is learning from the **consequences** of actions. Actions which have a good outcome through **positive** (reward) or **negative** (removal of something bad) **reinforcement** will be repeated. Actions which have a bad outcome (**punishment**) will not be repeated. Some examples include:

a) Maintaining **phobias** — we get anxious around phobic stimuli (heights, spiders etc) and avoid them. This removes the anxiety, which acts as negative reinforcement.

b) **Bulimics** feel guilt and disgust, so make themselves sick, removing these feelings in negative reinforcement.

c) **Anorexics** desire to lose weight, or to have more control of their life, so not eating is positive reinforcement.

Behavioural Therapies are Based on **Changes** Through **Conditioning**

Behaviourists try to identify what **reinforces** current behaviours and try to change this through conditioning.

1) Behavioural therapies can use **classical conditioning** to change behaviour:

Aversion therapy — An undesirable behaviour or stimulus can be associated with an **unpleasant response**.

Systematic desensitisation — A phobic can be **gradually** introduced to the feared object.

2) **Operant conditioning therapies** are often used in psychiatric hospitals. They control abnormal behaviour by removing the reinforcements which maintain the behaviour, and giving new reinforcements for better behaviour.

The Behavioural Model Has **Strengths** and **Weaknesses**

Strengths:

1) It is a **scientific** approach — it has clear **testable** concepts, which have been supported in many experiments.

2) Behavioural **therapies** can be very **effective** for treating phobias, eating disorders, obsessions and compulsions.

Weaknesses:

1) It cannot explain all behaviours because it neglects:

a) The influence of **genetics** and **biology** — how survival value and brain functioning affect behaviour.

b) The influence of **cognitions** — how thought processes contribute to disorders.

2) Behavioural therapies are **not effective** for **all** disorders, e.g. conditioning does not cure schizophrenia. Also, the procedures sometimes raise **ethical** issues, e.g. aversion therapy may be quite distressing.

The Cognitive Model of Abnormality

Another model you've got to learn. And if more models are right, that means they're all a bit wrong...

The Cognitive Model of Abnormality Concentrates on *Thoughts* and *Beliefs*

The cognitive model assumes that behaviours are controlled by thoughts and beliefs. So, irrational thoughts and beliefs cause abnormal behaviours. A few different versions of the model have been suggested:

Ellis (1991) — The 'ABC model' claims that disorders begin with an **activating event (A)** (e.g. a failed exam), leading to a **belief (B)** about why this happened. This may be rational (e.g. 'I didn't prepare well enough'), or irrational (e.g. 'I'm too stupid to pass exams'). The belief leads to a **consequence (C)**. Rational beliefs produce adaptive (appropriate) consequences (e.g. more revision). Irrational beliefs produce maladaptive (bad and inappropriate) consequences (e.g. getting depressed).

Beck (1963) — Beck identified a 'cognitive triad' of negative, automatic thoughts linked to **depression**: negative views about **themselves** (e.g. that they can't succeed at anything), about the **world** (e.g. that they must be successful to be a good person) and about the **future** (e.g. that nothing will change).

Cognitive Therapies Try to Change *Faulty Cognitions*

Cognitive therapies assume that we can treat psychological disorders by changing the original faulty thoughts and beliefs.
1) The therapist and client **identify** the client's faulty **cognitions** (thoughts and beliefs).
2) They then try to work out whether the cognitions are true, e.g. is it true that they always fail at what they do?
3) Together, they then set **goals** to think in more positive or adaptive ways, e.g. focusing on things the client has succeeded at and trying to build on them.

An example of this is Meichenbaum's **Stress Inoculation Training (S.I.T)**, developed to reduce stress (see page 31).

The Cognitive Model, Surprise Surprise, Has *Strengths* and *Weaknesses*

Strengths:
1) The cognitive model offers a **useful** approach to disorders like depression and anorexia. This is because it considers the role of **thoughts** and **beliefs**, which are greatly involved in problems like depression.
2) Cognitive therapies have often **successfully treated** depression, anxiety, stress and eating disorders.

Weaknesses:
1) Faulty cognitions may simply be the **consequence** of a disorder rather than its cause. For example, depression may be caused by a chemical imbalance in the brain, which causes people to think very negatively.
2) Cognitive therapies may take a long **time** and be **costly**. They may be more effective when **combined** with other approaches, e.g. cognitive-behavioural methods.

Practice Questions

Q1 How may classical conditioning explain abnormal behaviour?
Q2 Give an example of how operant conditioning could explain behaviour.
Q3 Explain a criticism of the behaviourist model of abnormality.
Q4 Explain the ABC model of abnormality.
Q5 Describe what happens in cognitive therapy.

Exam Questions

Q1 Explain an assumption of the behaviourist approach to abnormality and give a criticism of this approach. [6 marks]

Q2 Outline the assumptions of the cognitive approach to the causes and treatment of abnormality. [6 marks]

I think I'm mentally ill, therefore I am...

What's a bit confusing is that all these theories make some sense — you read them and think, 'So that's what it's all about, I get it now!' But then you read the next one and think the same thing... A second later you realise they can't both be true. Well, they can sort of both be true, but just not universally.

Critical Issue: Eating Disorders

Eating disorders are examples of psychological abnormalities. These pages show how different theories deal with them.

Anorexia Nervosa is an Eating Disorder

There are four main characteristics of anorexia:

1) **Anxiety** about getting fat, even when very underweight.
2) A **distorted body image** — **feeling fat**, even when they are very thin.
3) **Body weight** is less than 85% of what it should be for the person's age, height and build.
4) Female sufferers have further problems — their **periods stop**, or never start, depending on their age. The absence of **three or more** consecutive periods can indicate anorexia.

There are Loads of Suggested Causes for Anorexia

Genetic Factors Have Been Suggested

Holland et al investigated the possibility of **genetics** playing a part in anorexia:

Holland et al (1988) — genetic vulnerability to anorexia nervosa.

Method:	The participants were 45 sets of twins where at least one twin had had anorexia. They were interviewed on eating habits, body satisfaction and eating disorders in relatives.
Results:	In identical twins, **56%** both suffered from anorexia, whereas in non-identical twins, **5%** were both sufferers. There was also significantly more anorexia in the twins' **relatives** than in the normal population.
Conclusion:	There may be a **genetic vulnerability** for anorexia nervosa, which is triggered by environmental conditions.
Evaluation:	The results could perhaps be explained by the **environment** instead of genetics — maybe identical twins are treated more similarly than non-identical twins. It is also possible that twins **imitate** each other's behaviour, which might be more common in identical twins.

Biochemical Factors Have Been Suggested

1) **Fava et al (1989)** suggested a link between anorexia and increase in the levels of the neurotransmitters **serotonin** and **noradrenaline**.
2) **Antidepressants** work on people with eating disorders, suggesting an underlying **biochemical** problem.
But... It has been suggested that biochemical changes are actually a **consequence** of self-starvation, rather than a cause of it. **Fichter and Pirke (1995)** starved normal individuals and found changes in neurotransmitter and hormone levels, thus suggesting that they are a consequence, not a cause.

Brain Abnormalities Have Been Suggested

1) Parts of the **hypothalamus** control the release of hormones that regulate **hunger**.
2) **Garfinkel and Garner (1982)** suggested that anorexics have disturbed functioning in the hypothalamus.
But... This disturbed functioning may be a **consequence** rather than a cause of the anorexia. Also, **post-mortems** have not shown any problems or lesions in this area.

Psychological Factors Have Been Suggested

1) Freud's **psychodynamic theory** suggests that anorexics stop eating in order to avoid the adult body shape and so remain pre-pubescent. In this way, they can avoid the anxieties related to adulthood and sexual maturity.
2) **Bruch (1980)** suggested a psychodynamic approach based on **poor parenting**. If the child's signals are never properly responded to, the child never feels in control. Anorexia is a way of exerting control over their life.
3) Anorexia can be explained through **classical conditioning**. Eating might become associated with anxiety, as eating too much leads to unattractiveness. So losing weight reduces anxiety. It could also be **operant conditioning** — there might be reinforcement in the form of more attention for being slimmer.
4) The **cognitive approach** blames anorexia on **faulty belief systems** — simply not 'seeing' the huge weight loss.
5) **Becker (1999)** interviewed Fijians 3 years after they started receiving TV. She found that there was a strong increase in teenage girls who thought they were too fat. There was also an increase in eating disorders which she believed were due to the prevalence of **western media images**, linking beauty with slimness.

Critical Issue: Eating Disorders

Bulimia Nervosa is also an Eating Disorder

There are **four main characteristics** of bulimia:

1) The sufferer will **binge eat** — eating excessively without self-control (e.g. eating ten bars of chocolate non-stop).
2) The sufferer then tries to prevent weight gain through certain unhealthy behaviours, e.g. **self-induced vomiting**, **excessive exercise**, **laxative use**, **missing meals**.
3) They will **evaluate** themselves excessively on their **body image.**
4) The **binge-purging** behaviour will happen at least **twice a week** or more, over a three month period.

Bulimia is a **different condition** from anorexia — bingeing and purging are not the same as starving.

*There are also Loads of Suggested **Causes** for Bulimia*

Biological Factors Have Been Suggested

1) Bulimia has been linked to **low serotonin** levels (as opposed to high levels in anorexia). Being the opposite to levels in anorexics makes sense seeing as anorexics starve themselves and bulimics **binge**.
2) Eating lots of carbohydrate-rich, starchy foods can improve the **mood** of people with **low serotonin** levels. But, **Barlow and Durand (1995)** found that when bulimics binge, they did not focus specifically on carbohydrate-rich foods.
3) There might be a genetic link — **Kendler et al (1991)** carried out a twin-study and found that when one twin was bulimic, the other twin was also bulimic in **23%** of identical twins, and **9%** of non-identical twins.

Psychological Factors Have Been Suggested

1) The **behaviourist approach** suggests that bingeing is reinforcing because it provides a sense of indulgence. However, it causes anxiety which purging then reduces, so both bingeing and purging are **reinforced**.
2) A **cognitive theory** suggests that people with bulimia tend to **overestimate** their actual body size and want their body to be smaller than most people do. This is **distorted thinking** and **cognitive bias**.
3) The **psychodynamic theory** suggests that bulimia may be a result of repressed **childhood abuse**. Bulimia is therefore a way of both **punishing** the body and expressing **self-disgust**.
4) **Ruderman's (1986) disinhibition hypothesis** is about losing restraint. If bulimics feel they've overeaten, they think they've done the damage so they may as well carry on eating, and so binge — they've lost control. Afterwards, they feel guilt and disgust and so to get control back, they purge the food from their bodies.

Practice Questions

Q1 List four characteristics of anorexia nervosa.
Q2 Describe the findings of Holland et al.
Q3 Explain Freud's theory of anorexia.
Q4 List four characteristics of bulimia nervosa.
Q5 What is the disinhibition hypothesis?

Exam Questions

Q1 Critically evaluate biological explanations for anorexia nervosa. [18 marks]

Q2 Critically evaluate biological and psychological explanations for bulimia nervosa. [18 marks]

Every branch of psychology has a different explanation — great...

Anorexia and bulimia are very serious disorders. If untreated, anorexics can eventually starve themselves to death. We all want to look good, and a lot of us want to be thinner, but that doesn't mean there's anything wrong with us. It's when things get out of hand, when thoughts and feelings get too extreme and we start risking our health that it's wrong.

Conformity and Minority Influence

A few quick definitions to get you started — don't read on till you know them. **Conformity** *and majority influence mean the same thing — a small group or individual being influenced by a larger or dominant group.* **Compliance** *means publicly changing behaviour in line with the majority.* **Acceptance** *means changing your beliefs and internalising the majority's views.*

Many **Studies** Have Been Carried Out into **Conformity**

1) Sherif researched whether people are influenced by others in **an ambiguous task** (where the answer isn't clear):

Sherif (1935) — conformity and the autokinetic effect

Method:	The autokinetic effect (where a still point of light in the dark appears to move) was used in this experiment. Participants were shown a still point of light in the dark, and estimated how far it moved, first on their own and then in groups.
Results:	When alone, participants developed their own stable estimates (personal norms). In the group, judgements gradually became closer and closer until a **group norm** developed — an estimate they agreed on.
Conclusion:	Participants were influenced by the estimates of other people. Estimates converged because participants used information from others to help them.

2) Psychologists therefore wondered whether people conform to a majority's incorrect answer in **an unambiguous task**:

Asch (1956) — conformity on an unambiguous task

Method:	In groups of 7 or 8, participants judged line lengths (shown below) by saying out loud which comparison line (1, 2 or 3) matched the standard line. Each group contained only one real participant. The others were confederates (who acted like real participants but were really helping the experimenter). The real participant always went last or last but one, so they heard the others' answers before giving theirs. Each participant did 18 trials. On 12 of these (the **critical trials**) the confederates all gave the same wrong answer.
Results:	In the control trials, participants gave the wrong answer **0.7%** of the time. In the critical trials, participants **conformed** to the majority (gave the same wrong answer) **37%** of the time. **75%** conformed at least once. Afterwards, some participants said they didn't really believe their answers, but didn't want to look different.
Conclusion:	In the control group (where no confederates gave wrong answers) the error rate was 0.7%, so the task was easy to get right. But 37% were wrong on the critical trials — because they conformed to the majority to fit in.

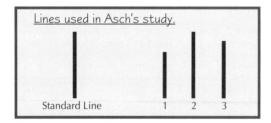

Lines used in Asch's study.   Standard Line   1   2   3

Seating plan for Asch's study. The real participant was always in position 7 or 8 and the others were confederates.   Stimulus Display

3) A very interesting experiment was carried out to see if people conformed to **assigned roles** (prisoner or guard):

Zimbardo et al (1973) — Stanford prison experiment

Method:	Male students were recruited to act as either guards or prisoners in a mock prison. Volunteers were screened and only 'well-balanced' people took part. They were randomly given the roles of prisoner or guard.
Results:	Initially, guards tried to assert their authority and prisoners resisted by sticking together. The prisoners became more passive and obedient, demonstrating 'learned helplessness' (see p32), and guards invented nastier punishments. The experiment was abandoned early because some prisoners became very distressed.
Conclusion:	Guards and prisoners adopted their social roles quickly. Zimbardo claims this shows **that our social role can influence our behaviour**, because well-balanced men became unpleasant and aggressive in the role of guard. However, individual differences played a part as not all the participants behaved according to their social roles.

Conformity and Minority Influence

An example of minority influence is the **Suffragettes**, a group campaigning for women's right to vote.
At the time, they didn't have widespread support, but gradually they influenced the majority to accept their ideas.

Moscovici et al (1969) Investigated Minority Influence

Moscovici et al (1969) — When is a blue slide green?

Method: This study is a bit like Asch's study (on the previous page).

There were 6 women in each group and 2 of these (the minority) were confederates (people who acted like real participants but were really helping the experimenter).

They were all given eye-tests, so participants knew the others weren't colour-blind.

Each person made a judgement out loud about the colour of 36 slides, which were various intensities of blue.

The error rate in the control group (where there were no confederates) was only 0.25% — so the task was really easy and the slides did look blue.

There were two experimental conditions:

— The '**inconsistent**' condition where confederates said 'green' for 24 of the 36 slides.

— The '**consistent**' condition where confederates said 'green' for all 36 slides.

Results: Inconsistent condition — real participants said green like the confederates for **1.25%** of the slides.

Consistent condition — real participants said green for **8.42%** of the answers.

32% conformed at least once in this condition.

Conclusion: Minorities can influence majorities. When the minority gave incorrect answers the majority were more likely to give 'green' as their answer too.

The effect is much smaller than in majority influence (conformity) studies, but there **is** an effect.

A consistent minority (both of them always said 'green') were more influential than an inconsistent one.

Evaluating the study:

1) **Ecological validity:** This study uses an **artificial task** and also the participants' **decisions don't have any major consequences**. Therefore the behaviour we see might not reflect how people are influenced by minorities in real life.

2) **Unrepresentative sample:** Moscovici et al used female students as participants, so it would be **wrong to generalise** these findings to all people — they only tell us about the behaviour of female students.

Practice Questions

Q1 What is the difference between compliance and acceptance?
Q2 In Sherif's study, what happened to the participants' judgements when making their estimates in a group?
Q3 What was the percentage of conformity on the critical trials in Asch's study?
Q4 What is a confederate?
Q5 In the study by Moscovici et al, in what condition were the minority most influential?
Q6 Why was the sample in the study by Moscovici et al unrepresentative?

Exam Questions

Q1 Explain the terms 'majority influence' and 'minority influence'. [6 marks]

Q2 Describe the findings and conclusions of one study of majority influence. [6 marks]

If enough people say this page is good — you'll start to believe it...

It seems unbelievable that just by hearing a few people say a blue tile is green, you will actually start to go along with them and say it is green yourself. Mind you, we've all been there — bands you hate that everyone else likes, people who annoy you but everyone else thinks is cool... We all feel that need once in a while to conform to the majority — or even a minority.

Conformity and Minority Influence

How much we conform and the influence of different groups on us is affected by lots of factors. And here are some lists of those factors — it may not make the most exciting reading, but it should be quite easy to learn.

Four Factors Affect Conformity

1) **Group Size**

You might **expect** that the bigger the majority is, the more influential it will be. To test this, **Asch (1951)** conducted his conformity experiment with different numbers of confederates as the majority.

With only **two confederates**, the real participant **conformed on only 13%** of the critical trials. With **three confederates**, conformity rose to **33%**. There was little change to conformity rates after that — no matter how big the majority group got. So, the **size of the majority does affect conformity, but only up to a point.**

2) **Gender**

Research findings have suggested that **females conform more than males**. It has been suggested that this is because **women** tend, more than men, to be **socially orientated** and focus on **interpersonal goals** (like getting on with people).

However, **Eadly & Carli (1981)** argue that it may be because **male researchers** use tasks that are more familiar to men (so they don't need to look to others as much for help). This could explain their finding that male researchers are more likely than female researchers to find female participants higher on conformity. This is an example of **gender bias**.

3) **Personality**

It seems plausible that some people are **more confident** and **resist conforming** to the majority more than others.

Asch (1956) suggested that people with **low self-esteem** (few positive feelings about themselves) **conform more**. He also found that students in his studies conformed less than non-students, and suggested that **higher IQ might be related to lower levels of conformity**.

4) **Status and knowledge**

If someone is of **high status** (e.g. your boss) or has **lots of knowledge** (e.g. a professor), they might be more influential, and so people will conform to their opinions more.

Adverts often use this technique so that their message has more influence — for example, getting a scientist to explain how good a washing powder is. Their **expertise** is influential.

People Conform for Two Main Reasons

1) **Informational influence:**

This is where a person looks to others for **information** when they're not sure how to behave. If you're in an unfamiliar situation or aren't sure of the answer, you might be influenced by someone else's behaviour or opinion.

This is the sort of social influence we saw in **Sherif's study**, where the task was ambiguous. Participants were informed by other people's estimates, which helped them with their judgements.

2) **Normative influence:**

This is where a person conforms to the **group norms**, so that they fit in and **appear 'normal'**.

Going against the majority might lead to exclusion or rejection from the group. They don't have to believe the majority's opinion or agree with their behaviour — they just have to appear 'normal'. People conform to normative influence so that they don't look different or stand out in a crowd.

This is the sort of influence we saw in **Asch's study**, where the right answer was obvious — an unambiguous task. Giving the wrong answer meant the participant didn't look different in the group.

Conformity and Minority Influence

Moscovici Identified Four Factors That Affect Minority Influence

Minority influence works by **converting the majority** to the **minority's belief**.
Moscovici (1985) said **conversion** (or **acceptance**) is more likely under the following conditions:

1) **Consistency** — A minority that consistently sticks to its belief is more influential.
   We saw this effect in Moscovici et al's blue slide study (see page 45).

2) **Flexibility** — A minority must **not seem too rigid** or stubborn. If a minority is unwilling
   to listen to alternative viewpoints, their own opinions are less likely to be influential.

3) **Commitment** — A minority must be **committed to its opinion and act on it**.
   For example, the Suffragettes showed commitment to their cause and made sacrifices for it.
   They were more influential because of this.

4) **Relevance** — A minority whose views are **in line with the general social trend**
   are more influential than a minority who are 'going against the grain'.

   For example, the current social trend is towards recycling and preserving resources.
   So these days it would be easier to influence your friends to recycle glass, cans and paper,
   than for someone to influence their friends to be 'green' 30 years ago.

Other **Factors** also Make People **Give In** to Minority Influence

Group Identification — We Identify With Someone **More** When We Have Something in Common

You might feel you are more similar to a person who goes to the same school as you, who is the same sex or who supports
the same team. You will therefore be more likely to accept an opinion from them than from someone very different.

Maass et al (1982) asked a straight audience to listen to a message on gay rights.
It was **more influential** if the message came from a **straight minority** and **less influential** coming from a **gay minority**.
They concluded that the audience **identified** more with the straight minority than with the gay minority.

Social Cryptoamnesia Explains how a **Minority Opinion** Can Become a **Majority Opinion**

Even when people convert their opinion to the minority's belief, they may not express it publicly, because they don't
want to stand out from the majority. A minority opinion might become a majority opinion by **social cryptoamnesia**:

1) The minority's view may change people's minds **privately**, but until the **social climate** changes too,
   these people may not become a majority group.

2) Minority views take time to affect things. During this time people forget where the opinion came
   from in the first place (the strange or deviant minority) and so the ideas themselves seem less extreme or strange.

3) They become **accepted** and ultimately end up as the **majority view**.

Practice Questions

Q1   According to Asch's findings, how does the size of the majority group affect the level of conformity?
Q2   What aspects of personality make a person more likely to conform?
Q3   Which study showed informational influence, and what is it?
Q4   Which study showed normative influence, and what is it?
Q5   What are the four factors, identified by Moscovici, that make conversion to a minority view more likely?
Q6   How might group identification affect minority influence?

Exam Questions

Q1   Outline two explanations of why people conform to a majority.   [6 marks]

Q2   Outline two ways in which a minority can become more influential.   [6 marks]

Imagine a bald man on a shampoo ad — no expertise, no influence...

*You were warned that there were going to be a lot of lists. At least the facts broken down like this should be easier to
understand. The main point to learn is that the influence of different groups and whether people conform to these views
depends on lots of different factors — then you just need to learn all those different lists of factors.*

Obedience to Authority

Obedience means acting in response to a direct order (usually from authority). Some people have problems doing this, but if an organisation or society is to work, many believe obedience is necessary.

Many Psychologists Have **Investigated** Obedience

1) Milgram studied how far people will obey authority, even when that means hurting someone else:

Milgram (1963) — the original 'remote learner' experiment

Method: 40 men from a range of occupations volunteered for a study about 'learning and memory'. The participant and a confederate (acting like a participant, but really helping the experimenter) drew lots to decide who would be the teacher and learner. The draw was fixed — the participant was always the teacher.

In the next room, the confederate was seemingly wired to an electric shock generator. The participant experienced an example shock of 45 volts before the experiment began. The participant taught the learner word-pairs. Every time the learner answered incorrectly the participant had to administer an increasing level of shock, from 15 V up to 450 V. (N.B. The learner didn't actually receive any shocks — he just acted like he did.) By each voltage level, there was a description of the shock, with things like 'slight shock', 'moderate shock' and 'danger: severe shock'. On 450 V, there was 'XXX'. At 300 V, the learner asked to be let out, and said he couldn't stand the pain. Above 300 V, the learner didn't respond.

If the participant stopped, they were ordered to continue by the experimenter in a lab-coat.

Results: It was predicted that around 1% would administer the highest shock. In fact, 65% of participants administered 450 V ('XXX') and none stopped before 300 V. Many participants showed signs of stress during the experiment.

Conclusion: Ordinary people obey orders even when they are acting against their conscience and hurting someone else.

Some of Milgram's variations on this experiment	Percentage administering 450 volts
Male participants	65%
Female participants	65%
Learner's protests can be heard	62.5%
Experiment run in seedy offices	48%
Learner in same room as particpant	40%
Authority (experimenter) in another room, communicating by phone	23%
Other teachers (confederates) refuse to give shock	10%
Other participant (a confederate) gives shock instead	92.5%

2) Hofling investigated whether nurses would break hospital rules to obey a doctor:

Hofling et al (1966) — obedience in nurses

Method: Nurses working in a hospital were phoned by an unknown doctor and asked to administer a drug to a patient. The doctor said he'd sign the paperwork when he arrived. To obey this request, nurses would have to break some hospital rules — taking telephone instructions from unknown doctors and administering drugs without completed paperwork were not permitted. Also, the dosage requested was twice the maximum on the label.

Results: 21 out of the 22 nurses obeyed the doctor and prepared the medication (they were stopped before they administered it). They said they were often given telephone instructions and doctors got annoyed if they refused.

Conclusion: In this real-life setting, levels of obedience to authority were high.

3) Meeus and Raaijmakers used interviews to test obedience:

Meeus & Raaijmakers (1995)

Method: Participants were asked to conduct interviews to test job applicants' reactions to stress. The applicants were really trained confederates. During the interview, the participants were prompted to deliver 15 'stress remarks', designed to inflict increasing levels of psychological harm. The confederates acted confidently at first, but then broke down as the stress remarks were delivered, eventually begging the interviewer to stop.

Results: Despite recognising the distress of the applicant, 22 of the 24 participants delivered all 15 stress remarks.

Conclusion: A high percentage were prepared to inflict psychological harm in this realistic, face-to-face situation.

Obedience to Authority

Obedience Research Has Been *Questioned*

1) **Ethical issues:**

Meeus and Raaijmakers caused their participants **psychological distress**.

All the experiments on the opposite page used **deception** (not telling participants what the study was really about or that they are in a study at all), so participants couldn't give **informed consent**.

If deceived, it is important to **debrief** participants (tell them the true nature of the study). Milgram's debrief was quite extensive, including being reunited with the 'learner'. Maybe he wasn't such a swine after all.

And no participants in these studies were informed of their **right to withdraw** from the experiment. In fact, in Milgram's and Meeus & Raaijmakers' procedure, participants were prompted to continue when they wanted to stop. I take it back, Milgram was a monster.

2) **Issues of validity:**

Experimental (internal) validity:

Whether Milgram's experiment really measured obedience is debatable. Some people claim that participants didn't really believe they were inflicting electric shocks — that they were just playing along with the **experimenter's expectations** (showing **demand characteristics**). But Milgram claimed participants' **stressed reactions** showed they believed the experimental set-up.

Hofling et al's nurses didn't know they were in an experiment, so it measured real obedience — this study has high experimental validity.

Ecological (external) validity:

Milgram's participants did a task that they were unlikely to encounter in real life (shocking someone). This is not real-life behaviour, therefore the study **lacks ecological validity**.

Real-life obedience is seen in Hofling et al's study — it has **more ecological validity**.

Milgram's Experiment Showed *Factors Affecting Obedience*

Proximity of the victim: Milgram's results suggest an important factor was the **proximity (closeness) of the learner**. In the 'remote learner' condition, 65% gave the maximum shock. This dropped to 40% with the learner in the same room and 30% when the participant had to put the learner's hand onto the shock plate. Proximity makes the learner's suffering harder to ignore.

Proximity of the authority: When the authority figure gave prompts by phone from another room, obedience rates dropped to 23%. When the authority isn't close by, their orders are easier to resist.

Presence of allies: When there were 3 teachers (1 participant and 2 confederates), the real participant was less likely to obey if the other two refused to obey. Having allies can make it easier to resist orders than when you're on your own.

Practice Questions

Q1 What is obedience?
Q2 Outline the procedure of Milgram's experiment.
Q3 In Milgram's original ('remote learner') experiment, what percentage of participants gave the maximum shock?
Q4 What is meant by 'proximity' and why is it a factor in obedience?
Q5 Outline the ethical issues of obedience research.

Exam Questions

Q1 Explain what is meant by ecological validity. [6 marks]

Q2 Describe **two** criticisms of **one** study of obedience. [6 marks]

Pretty shocking results, don't you think?

There's a lot packed into these two pages, but it's pretty interesting stuff. If you were in a room and a scientist told you to give an electric shock to a guinea pig, would you do it — and would it be because you were obeying authority, or just cos you quite like the idea of shocking a guinea pig...? These questions all affect the validity of psychological testing.

Obedience to Authority

Here's a whole pile of facts about how and why all that obedience happens. Interesting stuff...

Milgram's Findings Tell Us About the **Psychological Processes** Of Obedience

Gradual Commitment Can Make Us More Obedient

1) Gradual commitment means agreeing to something gradually — in **small steps**. It makes it **harder to refuse** the next request. In Milgram's study, participants were asked to deliver only a 15 V shock at the start. This was gradually built up to very large shocks.

2) Participants might have been more **reluctant** to obey **if** they had been asked to deliver the 450 V shock at the start. They obeyed at the lower levels, so it was harder for them to justify disobeying the later requests. They could have thought, 'I've already delivered a 300 V shock and 315 isn't much more'.

3) Gradual commitment is also known as the '**foot-in-the-door effect**'. Once you've gone along with a minor request, the request could be gradually increased until you're doing something you might never have agreed to in the first place.

An **Agentic State** is When You're Acting For Someone Else

1) Milgram suggested that when we feel we're acting out the wishes of another person (being their agent), we feel **less responsible** for our own actions than if we were behaving normally — for ourselves.

2) This effect is seen in Milgram's studies. Some participants were concerned for the **welfare** of the learner and asked who would take **responsibility** if he were harmed. The experimenter (authority) took responsibility — often the participant would continue.

3) This **agentic state** was also in the experiment's set-up. The participants voluntarily entered a **social contract** (an obligation) with the experimenter to take part and follow the procedure of the study.

Mr Ramsbottom, the new chemistry teacher, naturally exuded the persona of a justified authority figure.

We See Some People as a **Justified Authority**

We are socialised to recognise the authority of people like **parents**, **police officers**, **doctors**, **teachers** etc.

These kinds of people are **justified authorities** — people who have the **right** to **tell us what to do** and so we are more likely to obey them.

We are more likely to act as the agent for someone who we think of as a justified authority.

When Milgram reran his study in some **run-down offices**, obedience rates were lower than when the study was run in the university.

So in the university situation, the experimenter's authority was higher because of the status of the university location.

Some Things Can Act as **Buffers**

1) **Buffers** are things that **protect us** — in this case **from the consequences of our actions**.

2) Milgram's participants were **more obedient** in conditions where they **could not see or hear** the victim receiving the shocks. When in the same room as the learner, there wasn't any buffer.

3) So... losing the buffer made it harder for Milgram's participants to act against their conscience and go along with someone's unjust orders to hurt the learner.

Obedience to Authority

We Can Draw **Conclusions** About the Factors Affecting **Resistance** to Obedience

The **situation** Can Make People **More** Resistant

More of Milgram's participants resisted orders if there were **other teachers present** who refused to obey.

> **Gamson et al (1982)** found that support can help people resist authority, particularly if the request is unreasonable or unjust. They studied a **group** of participants **who felt they were being manipulated**. Participants rebelled against the unjust authority figure. This happened through a process of **minority influence** (see page 45) — with one or two people resisting the authority's requests at first. This rebellion then spread to the whole group.
>
> **Conclusion:** The presence of **allies** and **collective action** seemed to help the participants in their resistance.

Things About the **Individual** Can Make People **More** Resistant

1) If an individual has a high level of **moral reasoning** (thinking about right and wrong) they may be more able to resist an order that goes against their conscience.

2) One of Milgram's participants had experienced a Second World War concentration camp. She **refused** to administer any level of shock, because she didn't want to inflict pain on another person.

3) Those who resisted may have still felt personally responsible — they weren't in an agentic state.

4) As individuals we can also feel that when we are **pushed too far** to obey we can resist by defying the authority.

5) If we feel that someone is trying to control us, or that a rule unjustly restricts our freedom, we may react by doing the opposite. This is also known as the '**boomerang effect**'.

Proximity is an Important Factor

Proximity means closeness.

> 1) **Proximity of victim:**
> It was **harder** for Milgram's participants to ignore the consequences of their actions when the learner was nearby. They were more likely to resist an order that went against their conscience.
>
> 2) **Proximity of authority:**
> It is **easier** to resist the orders from an authority figure if they are **not close by**. When Milgram's experimenter gave prompts over the phone, obedience rates were lower than when they were face to face with the participant.
>
> 3) **Presence of allies:**
> Milgram and Gamson et al have shown that the presence of someone else who is resisting orders makes it easier to resist obedience yourself. Supporters or allies can help us resist obedience.

There's more detail on this stuff on pages 48-49.

Practice Questions

Q1 What is another name for the 'foot-in-the-door effect'?

Q2 Why did obedience rates drop when Milgram's study took place in run-down offices?

Q3 What term describes when you act on someone else's behalf and don't feel as responsible for your actions?

Q4 Give an example of a buffer that reduced obedience rates in one of Milgram's studies.

Q5 What did Gamson et al conclude from their research on independent behaviour?

Exam Questions

Q1 Give two explanations of why people obey authority. [6 marks]

Q2 Describe two factors that may help people resist obedience. [6 marks]

My local nightclub is in the local train station — it's called Buffers*...

Some people may resist obedience because they decide that what authority is telling them to do is not the right thing to do morally. Others rebel because they just don't like people telling them what to do. In that respect, disobedience can be a positive or negative thing. Most people would agree however, that setting your teacher on fire is more negative than positive.

*This sounds like a rubbish joke about railway buffers —
but it's actually true and represents a terrible reflection on the state of rural night clubbing.

Critical Issue: Ethical Issues in Research

Ethics are standards about what is right and wrong, so an ethical issue is some dilemma about whether a study is acceptable and justified. Try to imagine yourself as a participant in the studies — if you would've been happy about taking part, how you'd have felt and if it would've had long-term effects on you.

The British Psychological Society (BPS) produces **Ethical Guidelines**

The British Psychological Society (BPS) has developed ethical guidelines to help psychologists resolve ethical issues in research and protect participants. They include advice on **deception**, **consent** and **psychological harm**.

Deception Means Misleading or Withholding Information from Participants

Asch (see page 44) deceived participants about his study's purpose and about the confederates who pretended to be real participants. He justified this — without deception the aim of this study could not be achieved. If deception has to be used, participants should be told the true nature of the research as soon as possible, during the debriefing.

BPS Guidelines for Deception

Deception should be avoided wherever possible and only be used when it's scientifically justified — when the study would be meaningless otherwise.

Deception shouldn't be used if it's likely that the participant will be unhappy when they discover the study's true nature.

Informed Consent Should be Given

Giving consent means **agreeing** to participate in a study. When a participant is told the research aim and procedure and then agrees to it — this is **informed consent**. They are fully informed before their decision to participate. If deception is used, participants **can't** give informed consent until they've been debriefed.

Asch's participants **did not** give informed consent when they agreed to take part. They were deceived about aspects of the study and didn't have enough information for an informed decision.

BPS Guidelines for Informed Consent

Participants should be given all the information they need to decide whether to participate in research and shouldn't be coerced or pressured.

Some people may not be able to give real informed consent — for example children. In these cases informed consent should be obtained from parents or guardians.

Psychological Harm Means Any **Negative Emotion** (e.g. Stress, Distress, Embarrassment)

Asch's participants may have experienced **stress** and were possibly **embarrassed** about being 'tricked' into conforming.

BPS Guidelines for Psychological Harm

Researchers have a responsibility to protect participants from physical and psychological harm during the study. Any risk of harm should be no greater than the participant might experience in their normal life.

There are Many **Ethical Issues** in Other Social Influence Research

1) **Zimbardo et al** (see page 44) got **limited consent** from his prison-study participants — they weren't told they'd be arrested at their home. This experience and conditions in the mock prison may have caused **psychological harm**.

2) **Milgram's participants** were **deceived** about the true purpose of the study and about the learner being shocked (see page 48). They couldn't give **informed consent** until after they were debriefed. Many showed signs of **stress** and were pressured (by the experimenter) to continue when they wanted to stop. They weren't protected from psychological harm. After the study, many participants said they **weren't sorry** they took part. But this doesn't mean that they weren't psychologically harmed by knowing they were willing to give strong electric shocks to someone.

3) **Hofling et al's participants** didn't know they were in a study until after they had participated (see page 48). They were **deceived** and didn't give **consent**. The nurses may have been **psychologically harmed**, having realised they were willing to break hospital rules and possibly harm a patient.

Critical Issue: Ethical Issues in Research

Confidentiality and Animal Rights are Also Ethical Issues

Confidentiality means keeping information private.

1) Participants should feel safe that any sensitive information, results or behaviour revealed through research won't be discussed with others.

2) Information obtained during a study should remain confidential unless the participant agrees for it to be shared with others.

3) The study's report shouldn't reveal information or data identifiable to an individual.

4) You shouldn't be able to tell who took part or what their individual data were — these should remain anonymous.

Research with non-human animals has caused much heated debate.

1) In support, people argue that animal research has provided valuable information for psychological and medical research. Some research designs couldn't have be conducted on humans — e.g. Harlow's study on attachment, where young monkeys were separated from their mothers and reared alone.

2) Some disagree with the idea of conducting research with non-human animals. They may argue that it's ethically wrong to inflict harm and suffering on animals, and obviously animals can't give consent to take part.

3) Some argue that it's cruel to experiment on animals that have a similar intelligence to humans, because they might suffer the same problems we would. It'd be OK to experiment on animals that are far less developed than us, but there is no point because they'll be too different from us to give results that apply to humans.

Ethical Guidelines Don't Solve All the Problems

1) One obvious limitation with ethical guidelines is that there may be researchers who **don't follow the guidelines** properly.

2) If a psychologist conducts research in an unacceptable way, they **can't be banned** from research (unlike a doctor who might be 'struck off' for misconduct).

3) Even when guidelines are followed, it may be **difficult to assess** things like **psychological harm** or to **fully justify the use of deception**.

4) Deciding whether the ends (benefits from the study) justify the means (how it was done and at what cost) is not straightforward either. This creates another dilemma for psychologists.

Practice Questions

Q1 What are ethics?
Q2 According to the British Psychological Society's ethical guidelines, when can deception be used?
Q3 If you have used deception, what should you do immediately after the study?
Q4 What does 'informed consent' mean?
Q5 For the issue of psychological harm, what level of risk is said to be acceptable in research?
Q6 Give one reason why ethical guidelines don't solve all the problems of ethical issues in psychological research.

Exam Questions

Q1 Describe how psychologists have dealt with ethical issues in social influence research. [6 marks]
Q2 Discuss the extent to which the ethical objections about social influence research are justified. [18 marks]

People question the ethics of keeping a man in a box above the Thames...*

Psychological experiments create many ethical dilemmas. Take Milgram's study — there's no doubting that the results reveal interesting things about how people interact. But do these results justify the possible psychological damage done to the participants? There's no right or wrong answer to this, but the BPS guidelines are there to address exactly this sort of issue.

*I question the ethics of letting him out.

Research Methods

There are various ways of studying behaviour and gathering data — all have their pros and cons...

Laboratory Experiments are Controlled and Scientific

1) An **experiment** is a way of conducting research in a **controlled** way.
2) The aim is to **control** all relevant variables except for **one key variable**, which is altered to see what the effect is. The variable that you alter is called the **independent variable** (see page 57).
3) Laboratory experiments are conducted in an **artificial setting**, e.g. Milgram's and Asch's studies (see pages 44-48).

Advantages

Control — effects of confounding variables (those that have an effect in addition to the variable of interest) are minimised.

Replication — can run the study again to check the findings.

Causal relationships — it's possible to establish whether one variable actually causes change in another.

Disadvantages

Artificial — experiments might not measure real-life behaviour (i.e. they may lack ecological validity).

Demand characteristics — participants may respond according to what they think is being investigated, which can bias the results.

Field Experiments are Conducted Outside the Laboratory

In **field experiments** behaviour is measured in a **natural environment** like a school, the street or on a train. A **key variable** is still altered so that its effect can be measured.

Advantages

Causal relationships — you can still establish causal relationships by manipulating the key variable and measuring its effect.

Ecological validity — field experiments are less artificial than those done in a laboratory.

Demand characteristics — avoided if participants don't know they're in a study.

Disadvantages

Less control — confounding variables may be more likely in a natural environment.

Ethics — participants didn't agree to take part, might experience distress and often can't be debriefed.

Natural Experiments Measure but Don't Control Variables

A **natural experiment** is a study that measures variables that **aren't** directly manipulated by the experimenter. For example, comparing behaviour in a single-sex school and a mixed school.

Advantages

Ethical — it's possible to study variables that it would be unethical to manipulate, e.g. are people less aggressive in a community without TV?

Disadvantages

Participant allocation — you can't randomly allocate participants to each condition, and so confounding variables (e.g. what area the participants live in) may affect results.

Rare events — some groups of interest are hard to find, e.g. a community that doesn't have TV.

Correlational Research Looks for Relationships Between Variables

Correlation means that two variables rise and fall together, or that one rises as the other falls — but **not** necessarily that one variable **causes** a change in the other, e.g. as age increases so might intelligence, but age doesn't cause intelligence.

Advantages

Causal relationships — these can be ruled out if no correlation exists.

Ethical — can study variables that would be unethical to manipulate, e.g. is there a relationship between number of cigarettes smoked and incidence of ill-health?

Disadvantages

Causal relationships — cannot be assumed from a correlation, which may be caused by a third, unknown variable.

Misinterpretation — sometimes the media (and researchers) infer causality from a correlation.

Naturalistic Observation — Observing but NOT Interfering

Advantages

Ecological validity — natural behaviour and no demand characteristics, as participant unaware of being observed.

Theory development — can be a useful way of developing ideas about behaviour that could be tested in more controlled conditions later.

Disadvantages

Extraneous variables — can't control variables that may affect behaviour.

Observer bias — observer's expectations may affect what they focus on and record. This means the reliability of the results may be a problem — another observer may have come up with very different results.

Ethics — you should only conduct observations where people might expect to be observed by strangers. This limits the situations where you can do a naturalistic observation.

Research Methods

Questionnaires — *Written, Face-to-Face, on the Phone, or via the Internet*

Advantages   **Practical** — can collect a large amount of information quickly and relatively cheaply.

Disadvantages

Bad questions — leading questions (questions that suggest a desired answer) or unclear questions can be a problem. Or you might miss out an important question, so the participant doesn't have the opportunity to give certain information.

Biased samples — some people are more likely to respond to a questionnaire, which might make a sample unrepresentative.

Self report — people sometimes want to present themselves in a good light (social desirability bias). What they say and what they actually think could be different, making any results unreliable.

Interviews — *More Like a **Conversation** than a Face-to-Face Questionnaire*

Structured interviews follow a fixed set of questions that are the same for all participants.
Unstructured interviews may have a set of discussion topics, but are less constrained about how the conversation goes.

Advantages

Rich data — detailed information, as there are fewer constraints than with a questionnaire. Unstructured interviews provide richer information than structured interviews.

Pilot study — a good way to gather detailed information before further investigation.

Disadvantages

Self report — can be unreliable and affected by social desirability bias (see questionnaires).

Impractical — conducting interviews can be time-consuming and requires skilled researchers.

Ethical Guidelines *Advise and Protect*

1)   Different research methods present different **ethical issues** — dilemmas about how acceptable such research is.

2)   **Ethical guidelines** have been developed by organisations like the British Psychological Society to **advise** researchers and **protect** participants, e.g. observational research should only be carried out where people can expect to be observed by strangers.

 Other ethical guidelines are discussed on pages 52-53.

3)   The ethical issues depend on the actual research method used:

Method	Possible Ethical Issues
Laboratory Experiment	Deception often used, making informed consent difficult.
Field Experiment	Deception often used, making informed consent difficult. May be difficult to offer debriefing if people leave the location. Observation must respect privacy.
Natural Experiment	Deception often used, making informed consent difficult. Confidentiality may be compromised if community identifiable.
Correlational Studies	Misinterpretation of results.
Naturalistic Observation	Informed consent a problem. Observation must respect privacy. Debriefing may be difficult if people leave the location.
Questionnaire Surveys	Confidentiality — especially around sensitive issues.
Interviews	Confidentiality — especially around sensitive issues.

Practice Questions

Q1   What advantage is gained by running an experiment 'in the field' rather than in the laboratory?

Q2   Describe a disadvantage of studies where correlational analysis is used.

Q3   What ethical considerations are important when conducting observational research?

Q4   Why might you get an unrepresentative sample when carrying out questionnaire-based research?

Q5   What is the difference between a structured and unstructured interview?

Field experiments — fine, if you're really that interested in grass...

*No research method is perfect — the one you choose to use is bound to be some kind of compromise. A quick warning about correlation — correlation means that two variables rise and fall together, or that one rises as the other falls — but that doesn't necessarily mean that a change in one variable **causes** a change in the other. No, no, no, no, no.*

Aims and Hypotheses

When research is conducted, the idea is to produce an **objective test** of something — i.e. a scientifically proven measurement of how people behave, not just someone's opinion. Well that's what I reckon...

Research Aims are Important

1) An **aim** is a statement of a study's purpose — for example Asch's aim might have been: 'To study majority influence in an unambiguous task'. (See page 44 for the detail of Asch's study.)

2) Research should state its aim **beforehand** so that it's **clear** what the study intends to investigate.

Hypotheses are Theories Tested by Research

Although the **aim** states the **purpose** of a study, it isn't usually **precise** enough to **test**. What is needed are clear statements of what is actually being tested — the **hypotheses**.

1) **RESEARCH HYPOTHESIS**

The **research hypothesis** is proposed at the beginning of a piece of research and is often generated from a theory. For example — Bowlby's research hypothesis was that maternal deprivation causes delinquency. (See page 17 for the detail of Bowlby's study.)

2) **NULL HYPOTHESIS**

The **null hypothesis** is what you are going to **assume is true** during the study. Any data you collect will either back this assumption up, or it won't. If the data **doesn't support** your null hypothesis, you **reject** it and go with your **alternative hypothesis** instead.

Very often, the null hypothesis is a prediction that there will be **no relationship** between key variables in a study — and any correlation is due to **chance**. (An example might be that there is no difference in exam grades between students who use a revision guide and students who don't.)

(Note: It's quite usual to have something you **don't actually believe** as your null hypothesis. You assume it **is** true for the duration of the study, then if your results lead you to reject this null hypothesis, you've **proved** it **wasn't true** after all.)

3) **EXPERIMENTAL HYPOTHESIS (or ALTERNATIVE HYPOTHESIS)**

If the data forces you to **reject** your null hypothesis, then you accept your **experimental (alternative) hypothesis** instead.

So if your null hypothesis was that two variables **aren't** linked, then your alternative hypothesis would be that they **are** linked. Or you can be more specific, and be a bit more precise about **how** they are linked, using **directional** hypotheses (see below).

4) **DIRECTIONAL HYPOTHESIS (also called ONE-TAILED)**

A hypothesis might predict a difference between the exam results obtained by two groups of students — a group that uses a revision guide and another group that doesn't.

If the hypothesis states which group will do better, it is making a **directional prediction**.

For example, you might say that students who use a revision guide will get **higher** exam grades than students who don't — this is a directional hypothesis.

Directional hypotheses are often used when **previous research findings** suggest which way the results will go.

5) **NON-DIRECTIONAL HYPOTHESIS (also called TWO-TAILED)**

A **non-directional hypothesis** would predict a difference, but wouldn't say which group would do better.

For example, you might just say that there will be a **difference** in exam grades between students who use a revision guide and students who don't — this is a **non-directional** hypothesis, since you're not saying which group will do better.

Non-directional hypotheses can be used when there is **little previous research** in the area under investigation, or when previous research findings are **mixed** and **inconclusive**.

Aims and Hypotheses

Some *Variables* are *Manipulated* by the Researcher — Others aren't

A **variable** is a quantity whose **value changes** — for example time taken to do a task, anxiety levels, or exam results. There are various different kinds of variable.

The *Independent Variable* is *Directly* Manipulated

1) An **independent variable** (**IV**) is a variable **directly manipulated** by the researcher.

2) In the example about students, exams and revision guides, there are two variables. One is 'whether or not a revision guide is used' (so this variable has only two possible values: yes or no). The other is the 'exam grade' (and this could have lots of possible values: A, B, C, D, E, N, U).

3) In this case, the **independent variable** is 'whether or not the students used a revision guide' — since this is **directly** under the control of the researcher.

The *Dependent Variable* is Only Affected *Indirectly*

1) The **dependent variable** (**DV**) is the variable that you think is **affected** by changes in the independent variable. (So the DV is **dependent on** the IV.)

2) In the exam grades example, the dependent variable is the 'exam grade'. The exam grade is dependent upon whether the revision guide was used (or at least, that's what's being **investigated**).

Extraneous Variables are *Extra* Things that *Might* Affect What You're Trying to *Measure*

1) Ideally in a study you'd keep all the variables **constant** and change just one (the **IV**) to see **what effect** it has on the **DV**. Unfortunately, sometimes this isn't done (or isn't possible).

2) An **extraneous variable** is any variable (other than the IV) that **could** affect what you're trying to measure.

3) For example, some students could sit exams at different times, use different revision guides, be different ages or genders. Any one of these could affect the exam results, so they would be **extraneous** variables.

Confounding Variables are Extraneous Variables that Have *Actually Had* an Effect

1) Ideally the **only** difference between groups in a study will be down to the IV under investigation — then any **difference** in the **DV** is caused by a **difference** in the **IV**.

2) However, one or more extraneous variables may also have affected the DV. If this is the case, it's called a **confounding variable**.

3) For example, if all the students in the group using revision guides were studying Physics and all the students not using them were doing Chemistry, there's possibly a **confounding** variable. If the group using the revision guide do better, it might be because it's easier to get a higher mark in Physics.

Practice Questions

Q1 What is a hypothesis?
Q2 What is the difference between a directional and non-directional hypothesis?
Q3 When would we reject the null hypothesis?
Q4 What is an independent variable?
Q5 What is a dependent variable?
Q6 Why does a confounding variable make it difficult to interpret differences found in results?

Aim to learn this page, I hypothesise you'll need it...

Remember, you assume the null hypothesis is true unless your data suggests otherwise — then you quickly switch allegiance to the alternative hypothesis instead. And remember, the IV is deliberately manipulated by the researcher. This might lead to an effect on the DV, but it's often a kind of indirect, knock-on effect. Yep, I agree — that's enough.

Research Design

Once you've got a theory, this is about how you'd actually go about researching...

The Research Design Must make the Hypothesis **Testable**

> **Research example** — does the presence of an audience help or hinder people doing the 'wiggly wire' task (moving a loop along a wire without touching it, and setting off the buzzer)?
>
> Based on previous research, we expect people to do this better without anyone watching them.

1) The IV (the variable being manipulated) is the presence or absence of an audience.

2) The DV (the variable being measured) is 'how well' the participants do on the task — but it must be testable. You need a **precisely defined** (or **operationalised**) DV, which should be **quantitative** wherever possible. An operationalised DV for this experiment might be 'the time taken to move the loop from one end of the wire to the other without setting off the buzzer'.

There are Three **Research Designs** that are Used Loads

1) An **independent measures design** means there are **different participants** in each group.

Here, for example, one group does the task *with* an audience and another group does it *alone*.

This avoids the problem that if all the participants did the test in both conditions, any improvement in performance might be due to them having two goes at the task (which would be a confounding variable).

Advantages	*Disadvantages*
No **order effects** — no one gets better through practice (**learning effect**) or gets worse through being bored or tired (**fatigue effect**).	**Participant variables** — differences between the **people** in each group might affect the results (e.g. the 'without audience' group may just have people who are better at the task — so we can't safely compare groups). **Number of participants** — **twice as many** participants are needed to get the same amount of data, compared to having everyone do both conditions.

2) A **repeated measures design** is where all participants do the task both **with** an audience and then **without**. You can compare the performances in each condition, knowing the differences weren't due to participant variables.

Advantages	*Disadvantages*
Participant variables — now the same people do the test in both conditions, so any differences between individuals shouldn't affect the results. **Number of participants** — **fewer** participants are needed to get the same amount of data.	**Order effects** — if all participants did the 'with audience' condition first, any improvements in the second condition could be due to **practice**, not the audience's absence. (But see **counterbalancing** on the next page.)

3) A **matched participants design** (also known as 'matched pairs') means there are different participants in each condition, but they're **matched** on important variables (like age, sex and personality).

For example, if a participant in one condition was a 20-year-old male, you'd also want a participant in the other condition to be a male aged around 20 with a similar personality.

Advantages	*Disadvantages*
No **order effects** — there are **different people** in each condition. **Participant variables** — important differences are minimised through **matching**.	**Number of participants** — need twice as many people compared to repeated measures. **Practicalities** — **time-consuming** and difficult to find participants who **match**.

It's Sometimes Good to Run a Small **Pilot Study** First

1) No piece of research is perfect. To help foresee problems, a small-scale **pilot study** can be run first.

2) This should establish whether the **design** works, whether **participants** understand the wording in **instructions**, or whether something important has been **missed out**.

3) Problems can be tackled before running the **main study**, which could save a lot of wasted **time** and **money**.

Research Design

Variables Can Be 'Controlled' so Their Unwanted Effects are Minimised

Counterbalancing (mixing up the order of the tasks) can solve **order effects** in **repeated measures** designs. Half the participants do the task **with** an audience **first** and **then without**. The others do the conditions **the other way round**. Any order effects would then be equal across conditions.

Random allocation (e.g. by drawing names out of a hat) means everyone has an **equal chance** of doing **either** condition. An **independent measures** study with, for example, more men in one group than the other could have a confounding variable. Any difference in performance may be due to **sex** rather than the real IV. Random allocation should ensure groups are **not biased** on key variables.

Extraneous variables can be controlled by: (i) keeping them **constant** for all participants (e.g. everyone does the task in the same place so distractions are similar),

(ii) eliminating them altogether (e.g. everyone does the task somewhere with no noise distractions).

Standardised instructions these should ensure the **experimenters** act in a similar way to all participants. Everything should be **as similar as possible** for all the participants, including each participant's **experience** in such studies.

Tests should be Internally and Externally Reliable

Internal Reliability

1) Is the measure consistent? **Split-half technique** can assess this. Questionnaire items are randomly split into **two groups**. If all participants score similarly on both halves, the questions measure the same thing.

2) Are you measuring what you **think** you're measuring? A way of assessing this is **predictive validity** — do the scores on your test predict actual performance? For example, a test to measure how good someone will be at management will have predictive validity if it picks out those people who go on to become good managers.

External Reliability

1) Is the measure stable over time or between people? This can be assessed by measuring **test-retest reliability** (does the same person always score similarly on the test?) or **inter-rater reliability** (do different assessors agree, i.e. do they both give the same score?)

2) Does the study tell us about **real-life** behaviour? This can be improved by using less artificial surroundings, e.g. field experiments or naturalistic observations.

Research should be designed with Ethical Issues in mind

Ethical guidelines assist researchers who have **ethical dilemmas** and should ensure that research is **acceptable** and participants are **protected**.

Practice Questions

Q1 Give one disadvantage of an independent measures design.

Q2 Give one design that overcomes the disadvantage you identified in Q1.

Q3 Give one disadvantage of a matched participants design.

Exam Questions

Choose an example of a famous piece of psychological research to answer these questions:

Q1 Identify the design used in this study. [2 marks]

Q2 Describe one conclusion that could be drawn from the findings in this study. [2 marks]

Q3 Describe one problem that may limit the validity of the conclusion you have identified in Q2. [3 marks]

Inter-test validity, no... split-rater ethics, no... oh sod it.... zzzzzzzzz...

There are a lot of details here, but they're really important. If you're not really careful when you design a piece of research, the results you get might not be worth the paper you end up writing them down on. Spending a little time thinking at this stage will all be worth it in the end — trust me.

Naturalistic Observation

Naturalistic observation is the collection of data by observing participants in their natural environments. This may seem pretty simple, but there are still lots of important design decisions to be made.

Making **Naturalistic Observations** Needs a Lot of Thought

Recording data

If you want **qualitative data** (e.g. words, pictures, etc.) you could just make **written notes**. But **video** or **audio recording** means that you have a **permanent** record, and also ensures no behaviours are missed.

Categorising behaviour

You must **define** the behaviours you aim to observe. For example, if you were going to observe children in a school playground to see how many behave aggressively, you'd have to decide **what counts as aggression**.

This involves giving an **operationalised definition** (i.e. some **specific, observable** behaviours). For example, you might say that *'aggression is any physical act made with the intention to harm another person – such as punching, kicking etc.'*

But you have to be careful not to **miss out** anything important otherwise your definition may not be valid, e.g. aggression can also be verbal.

Rating behaviour

The behaviours that you're interested in may be things that are a matter of **degree**, e.g. behaviours may be *very aggressive, mildly aggressive*, etc. — so you might need to use a rating scale to classify behaviour.

You could put each participant's behaviour into one of several **categories**, e.g. *not aggressive, mildly aggressive* or *very aggressive*.

Or you could use a **coding system** where each participant is given a **number** (e.g. between 1 and 10) to represent how aggressive they are, where a **higher score** indicates **more aggression**. However, you still have to **define** what kinds of behaviour are included for each number on the scale (e.g. 5 = *pushing* and 10 = *kicking or punching more than once*).

Behaviour rated in this way provides **quantitative data** (data in the form of **numbers**).

Sampling behaviour

You have to decide **how often** and for **how long** you're going to observe the participants. Two approaches are **event sampling** and **time-interval sampling**.

Event sampling — this is when you only record particular events that you're interested in (e.g. aggression shown by the children) and ignore other behaviours.

Time-interval sampling — if the behaviours occur over a long time period you might choose to observe for only set time intervals e.g. the first 10 minutes of every hour, or 10 minutes of each playtime the children have in a week. The time intervals could be chosen randomly.

Inter-observer reliability

Even after you've **defined** the behaviours you're interested in, you have to make sure that the observers are actually putting each participant in the **right category** or giving the **right rating**. This might involve **comparing** the data from two or more observers to make sure they're giving the **same** scores (i.e. that they are 'reliable').

Naturalistic Observation

And there's more...

Questionnaires *Need to be Designed* Carefully

There are various things you need to consider when designing a questionnaire for a survey.

1) **Type of data** — whether you want **qualitative data** and/or **quantitative data** will affect whether you ask **open** and/or **closed questions**.

   a) **Open questions** are questions such as *What kinds of music do you like?*
   The participant can reply in **any way**, and in as much detail as they want. This gives detailed, qualitative information, although it may be **hard to analyse**, as the participants could have given very different answers.

   b) **Closed questions** limit the answers that can be given, e.g. *Which do you like: Pop, Rock or neither?*
   They give **quantitative** data that is relatively **easy to analyse** — e.g. you can say exactly **how many** people liked each type of music. However, less detail is obtained about each participant.

2) **Ambiguity** — you have to avoid questions and answer options which are **not** clearly **defined**, e.g. *Do you listen to music frequently?* What is meant here by 'frequently'? — Once a day, once a week?

3) **Double-barrelled questions** — best not to use these, since a person may wish to answer **differently** to each part. For example, *Do you agree that modern music is not as good as the music of the 1960s and that there should be more guitar-based music in the charts?*

4) **Leading questions** — these are questions that **lead** the participant towards a particular answer. E.g. *How old was the boy in the distance?* They might have seen an older person, but by saying 'boy' you're leading them to describe the person as young. You're also leading them to think that the person was male, but they might not have been sure. (Leading questions are really important in eyewitness testimony — see pages 10-11.)

5) **Complexity** — whenever possible **clear English** should be used, avoiding **jargon**.
   However, if specialist terms are included, they should be clearly defined.
   (So the question *Do you prefer music written in unusual time signatures?* probably isn't ideal for most people.)

All of the Above Goes For Interviews *As Well*

But you also have to consider the following:

1) **How structured** the interview will be:
   Interviews can be very **informal** with **few set questions**, and new questions being asked **depending on** the participant's **previous answers**. This gives detailed qualitative data, which may be difficult to analyse.

   Alternatively, they may be more **structured**, with set questions and **closed answers**, giving **less detail** but being **easier to analyse**.

2) Using a **question checklist** — if the interview is structured, a checklist ensures that no questions are left out and questions aren't asked twice.

3) The behaviour or appearance of the **interviewer** — this could **influence** how the participants react.

Practice Questions

Q1   Explain the difference between quantitative and qualitative data.
Q2   How can behaviour be sampled in observational studies?
Q3   What is 'inter-observer reliability'?
Q4   Distinguish between open and closed questions.
Q5   Explain three of the issues involved in designing questionnaires and/or interviews.

Big Brother — *naturalistic observation at its finest...?*

This is all about observing behaviour that's as natural as possible. What you don't want is for people to put on an act just because they're aware that they're being watched — that defeats the object of doing the study in the first place. Makes you wonder about Big Brother — can they keep an act up for ten whole weeks, or do we actually get to see some natural stuff?

Selecting and Using Participants

In a study, you could ask everyone in the world some questions, but that's not really practical.
This is why in most cases it's best to survey just a sample of participants. But you have to be careful how you choose them.

Selecting a **Sample** of Participants Can Be Done in **Three Main Ways**

The part of a **population** that you're interested in studying (e.g. all the people in a particular city, or all people of a certain age or background) is called the **target group**. Usually you can't include everyone in the target group in a study, so you choose a certain **sample** of **participants** (or **Pp** for short).

This sample should be **representative**, i.e. it should reflect the variety of characteristics that are found in the target group. A sample that is unrepresentative is **biased**. There are various methods of selecting a sample:

RANDOM SAMPLING

This is when **every** member of the target group has an **equal chance** of being selected for the sample. This could be done by giving everyone in the target group a number and then getting a computer to randomly pick numbers in order to select the Pp.

Advantages: Random sampling is 'fair'. Everyone has an equal chance of being selected and the sample is **likely** to be representative.

Disadvantages: This method doesn't **guarantee** a representative sample — there's still a chance that some sub-groups in the target group may not be selected (e.g. people from a minority cultural group). Also, if the target group is large it may not be practical (or possible) to give everyone a number that might be picked. So in practice, completely random samples are rarely used.

OPPORTUNITY SAMPLING

This is when the researcher samples whoever is **available and willing** to be studied. Since many researchers work in universities, they often use opportunity samples made up of students.

Advantages: This is a **quick** and **practical** way of getting a sample.

Disadvantages: The sample is **unlikely** to be **representative** of a target group or population as a whole. This means that we can't confidently **generalise** the findings of the research. However, because it is **quick** and **easy**, opportunity sampling is **often used**.

VOLUNTEER SAMPLING

This is when people actively **volunteer** to be in a study by responding to a request for Pp advertised by the researcher, e.g. in a newspaper, or on a notice board. The researcher may then select only those who are **suitable** for the study. (This method was used by Milgram — see page 48.)

Advantages: If an advert is placed prominently (e.g. in a national newspaper) a **large number** of people may respond, giving more Pp to study. This may allow more **in-depth analysis** and **more accurate** statistical results.

Disadvantages: Even though a large number of people may respond, these will only include people who actually saw the advertisement — no one else would have a chance of being selected.
Also, people who volunteer may be more **co-operative** than others. For these reasons the sample is **unlikely** to be **representative** of the target population.

No method can <u>guarantee</u> a representative sample, but you should have confidence that your sample is (quite) representative if you want to <u>generalise</u> your results to the entire target group.

Selecting and Using Participants

Participants Sometimes **Act Differently** When They're Being **Observed**

Human Pp will usually be aware that they are being **studied**. This may mean they don't show their **true response**, and so their data may not be **valid** or **reliable**. Some of these effects are explained below...

1) **THE HAWTHORNE EFFECT**: If people are **interested** in something and in the attention they are getting (e.g. from researchers), then they show a more **positive** response, try **harder** at tasks, and so on.

    This means their results for tests are often **artificially high** (because they're trying harder than normal), which could make a researcher's conclusions **inaccurate**.

    The opposite effect may occur if the Pp are **uninterested** in the task.

2) **DEMAND CHARACTERISTICS**: This is when Pp look for **clues** to the aims of a study.

    If they think they realise what kinds of response the researcher is **expecting** from them, they may show that response to '**please**' the researcher (or they may **deliberately** do the **opposite**). Either way, the conclusions drawn from the study would be **inaccurate**.

3) **SOCIAL DESIRABILITY BIAS**: People usually try to show themselves in the **best possible light**.

    So in a survey, they may **not** be completely **truthful**, but give answers that are more **socially acceptable** instead (e.g. people may say they give more money to charity than they really do). This would make the results **less accurate**.

The **Researchers** Can **Affect** the Outcomes in **Undesirable ways**

The **reliability** and **validity** of results may also be influenced by the researcher, since he or she has **expectations** about what will happen. This can produce the following effects:

1) **RESEARCHER (or EXPERIMENTER) BIAS**: The researcher's **expectations** can influence how they **design** their study and how they **behave** towards the Pp, which may then produce **demand characteristics**.

    Also, their expectations may influence **how** they take **measurements** and **analyse** their data, resulting in errors that can lead, for example, to accepting a hypothesis that was actually false.

2) **INTERVIEWER EFFECTS**: The interviewer's **expectations** may lead them to ask only questions about what *they* are **interested** in, or to ask **leading questions**.

    Or they may **focus** on the aspects of the Pp's answers which **fit** their **expectations**.

    Also a Pp may react to the **behaviour** or **appearance** of an interviewer and then not answer truthfully.

Practice Questions

Q1 What is a biased sample?
Q2 What is a random sample?
Q3 Give a disadvantage of opportunity sampling.
Q4 Give an advantage of volunteer sampling.
Q5 What is the Hawthorne effect?
Q6 How may demand characteristics affect a study?
Q7 How may a researcher's expectations affect a study?

Volunteers needed for study into pain and embarrassment... (and stupidity)

In a study, you could survey everyone in the world, but it might be expensive and time-consuming. This is why in most cases it's better to survey just a sample of participants. But you have to be careful how you choose them. There's no point in going to your local club and surveying all the crazy dancing people, cos I bet down at the old folk's home they'd disagree.

Data Analysis

Data analysis may sound vaguely maths-like — but don't run for the hills just yet. It isn't too tricky...

Data From **Observations** Should be Analysed **Carefully**

1) If you've got **quantitative** data (i.e. numbers), you can use **statistics** to show, for example, the most common behaviours. (Quantitative data can be obtained by **categorising** and **rating** behaviour — see page 60.)

2) **Qualitative** data might consist of video or audio **recording**, or written **notes** on what the observers witnessed. Analysis of qualitative data is **less straightforward**, but it can still be done.

3) Whatever kind of data you've got, there are some important issues to bear in mind:

    a) There must be **adequate data sampling** to ensure that a **representative** sample of Pps' behaviour has been seen.

    b) **Language** must be used **accurately** — the words used to describe behaviour should be **accurate** and **appropriate** (and must have valid **operationalised definitions**). For example, it might not be appropriate to describe a child's behaviour as 'aggressive' if he or she is play-fighting.

    c) Researcher **bias** must be **avoided** — e.g. it's not okay to make notes *only* on events that **support** the researcher's theories, or to have a **biased interpretation** of what is observed.

The Same Goes For Data Obtained From **Interviews**

1) When **closed** questions are used as part of an interview's structure, **quantitative** data can be produced (e.g. the **number** of Pps who replied 'Yes' to a particular question). **Statistics** can then be used to further analyse the data.

2) When **open** questions are used, more **detailed**, **qualitative** data are obtained.

3) Again, whatever you've got, there are certain things you'll need to remember:

    a) **Context** — the **situation** in which a Pp said something, and the way they were **behaving** at the time, may be important. It may help the researcher understand **why** something was said, and give clues about the **honesty** of a statement.

    b) The researcher should clearly distinguish **what** was said by the Pp from **how** *they* interpreted it.

    c) **Selection** of data — a lot of **qualitative** data may be produced by an interview, which may be difficult for the researcher to **summarise** in a report. The researcher must **avoid bias** in selecting what to include (e.g. only including statements that support their ideas). The interviewees may be consulted when deciding **what** to include and **how** to present it.

    d) The interviewer should be aware of how *their* feelings about the interviewee could lead to **biased interpretations** of what they say, or how it is later reported.

And Likewise For Data From **Questionnaire Surveys**

1) Like observations and interviews, **surveys** can give you both **quantitative** and **qualitative** data, and so most of the points above are relevant to surveys as well.

2) Again, it's especially important to distinguish the **interpretations** of the **researcher** from the **statements** of the **participant**, and to be **unbiased** in selecting what to include in any report on the research.

3) However, the analysis of **written** answers may be especially difficult because the participant is not present to **clarify** any **ambiguities**, plus you don't know the **context** for their answers (e.g. what mood they were in, and so on).

Data Analysis

Qualitative Data Can Be Tricky to Analyse

Qualitative data are sometimes seen as 'of limited use' because they're difficult to analyse.
This is why they are often converted into quantitative data using content analysis.

CONTENT ANALYSIS

a) A representative sample of qualitative data is first collected — e.g. from an interview, printed material (newspapers, etc.) or other media (such as TV programmes).

b) Coding units are identified to analyse the data. A coding unit could be, for example, an act of violence, or the use of gender stereotypes (though both of these must be given valid operationalised definitions first — e.g. a definition of an 'act of violence').

c) The qualitative data are then analysed to see how often each coding unit occurs (or how much is said about them, etc.).

d) A statistical analysis can then be carried out. (Don't worry, you don't need to know how to do these for AQA A. Lucky so and so.)

ADVANTAGES OF QUANTIFYING DATA

1) It becomes easier to see patterns in the data, and easier to summarise and present it (see pages 70-71).

2) Statistical analysis allows statements regarding significance to be made.

DISADVANTAGES OF QUANTIFYING DATA

1) Care is needed to avoid bias in defining coding units, or deciding which behaviours fit particular units.

2) Qualitative data has more detail (context, etc.), which is lost when converted into numbers.

1) Because of the detail (and hence the insight) that qualitative data can give, some researchers prefer to avoid 'reducing' them to numbers.

2) Instead they analyse the data into categories or 'typologies' (e.g. sarcastic remarks, statements about feelings, etc.), quotations, summaries, and so on.

3) Hypotheses may be developed during this analysis, rather than being stated previously, so that they are 'grounded in the data'.

Quantitative Data Allow You to Make Statements Regarding Significance

1) There's always the chance that results might be due to chance rather than the variables of interest.

2) One advantage of quantifying data is that it allows you to use inferential statistics. These allow you to check whether results are likely to be due to chance. If the probability of the result being down to chance is sufficiently small, you say that a finding is significant.

Practice Questions

Q1 Distinguish between qualitative and quantitative data.
Q2 Why is data sampling an issue in observation studies?
Q3 Why is context important in analysing interview data?
Q4 How may bias occur in analysing interview or survey data?
Q5 Why may survey data be harder to analyse than interview data?
Q6 How is a content analysis done?

You must keep an open mind — but just don't let all the facts escape...

It's fairly obvious-ish, I guess, that qualitative data need to be analysed with an open mind — it's not OK to fit the facts to your theory... you have to fit your theory to the facts. The same goes for analysing quantitative data — it's not just a case of 'doing some maths' — you have to be sure you're not being biased in your interpretations. Keep an open mind...

Descriptive Statistics

Run for your lives... panic. This really looks like maths... Well, actually, it's not too bad. So calm down.

Descriptive Statistics — Just Say What You See...

1) **Descriptive statistics** simply describe the **patterns** found in a set of data.

2) Descriptive statistics uses the fancy term '**central tendency**' to describe an **average**. For example, the central tendency (average) for the height of a group of 18-year-old boys might be about 1.70 metres.

3) Measures of **dispersion** describe **how spread out** the data are.
   For example, the difference in height between the shortest 18-year-old boy and the tallest might be 35 cm.

There are 3 Measures of *Central Tendency* (AKA Average) You Need to Know

The Mean — *This is the 'Normal Average'*

You calculate the **mean** by **adding** all of the scores in a data set and then **dividing** by the number of scores.

$$\text{Mean} = \bar{X} = \frac{\sum X}{N}, \text{ where } \sum X \text{ is the sum of all the scores (and there are } N \text{ of them).}$$

Σ (pronounced 'sigma') just means you add things up.

Example: If you've got scores of 2, 5, 6, 7 and 10, then $\sum X = 30$ (since all the scores add up to 30), and $N = 5$ (since there are 5 of them)...

...so the **mean** is $\bar{X} = \dfrac{30}{5} = 6$.

For example, the scores 10, 40, 25, 20 and 650 have a mean of 149, which is not representative of the central tendency of the data set.

Advantages

a) It uses **all** the scores in a data set.

b) It's used in **further calculations** (e.g. standard deviation, see next page), and so it's handy to work out.

Disadvantages

a) It can be **skewed** (distorted) by extremely **high** or **low** scores. This can make it **unrepresentative** of most of the scores, and so it may be **misleading**. In these cases, it's best to not use the mean.

b) It can sometimes give an **unrealistically precise** value (e.g. the average home has 2.4 children — but what does 0.4 of a child mean...?)

The Median — *The **Middle Score** When the Data are Put in **Order***

Example: The **median** of the scores 4, 5, 10, 12 and 14 is **10**.

In this example there was one score in the middle. If there are two middle scores, add them together and then divide by 2 to get the median.

Advantages

a) It's relatively **quick** and **easy** to calculate.

b) It's **not** affected by extremely high or low scores, so it can be used on 'skewed' sets of data to give a '**representative**' average score.

Disadvantages

a) Not **all** the scores are used to work out the median.

b) It has **little further use** in data analysis.

The Mode — *The Score that Occurs **Most Often***

Example: The **mode** (or the **modal score**) of 2, 5, 2, 9, 6, 11 and 2 is 2.

If there are two scores which are most common then the data set is 'bi-modal'. If there are three or more scores which are most common then the data set is 'multi-modal'.

Advantages

a) It shows the **most common** or 'important' score.

b) It's always a result from the actual **data set**, so it can be a more **useful** or **realistic** statistic, e.g. the modal average family has 2 children not 2.4.

Disadvantages

a) It's not very useful if there are **several** modal values, or if the modal value is only **slightly** more common than other scores.

b) It has **little further use** in data analysis.

Descriptive Statistics

Measures of *Dispersion* Tell You How *Spread Out* the Data Are

There are two of these you should learn.

Range — *Highest Score Minus the Lowest Score*

Example: The range of the scores 6, 10, 35 and 50, is 50 – 6 = 44

> Note that (highest – lowest)+1 can also be used, so the range would then be = 45.

Advantage — it's **quick** and **easy** to calculate.

Disadvantage — it completely ignores the **central** values of a data set, so it can be misleading if there are very **high** or **low** scores.

1) The **interquartile range (IQR)** can be calculated to help **avoid** this problem.
2) First the **median** is calculated (this is sometimes called **Q2**).
3) Then the value **halfway** between the **median** and the **lowest score** is found (called the **lower quartile**, or **Q1**).
4) Then the value halfway between the **median** and the **highest score** is found (called the **upper quartile**, or **Q3**).
5) The **IQR = Q3 – Q1**.

> *Example*: 3, 3, **4**, 5, 6, **8**, 10, 13, **14**, 16, 19.
> There are 11 values, so
> median (Q2) = 6th value = 8.
> Then Q1 = 4, Q3 = 14,
> and so IQR = 14 – 4 = 10.

Standard Deviation — *Measures How Much Scores Deviate From the Mean*

$$s = \sqrt{\frac{\sum (X - \bar{X})^2}{N}}, \quad \text{where } s = \text{standard deviation}$$

Example: Scores = 5, 9, 10, 11 and 15. The mean = 10.
So the standard deviation is:

$$s = \sqrt{\frac{(5-10)^2 + (9-10)^2 + (10-10)^2 + (11-10)^2 + (15-10)^2}{5}} = 3.22$$

> A high standard deviation shows more variability in a set of data.

Advantage — **all** scores in the set are taken into account so it is **more accurate** than the range and it can be used in further analysis.

Disadvantage — it's **not** as quick or easy to calculate as the range.

Practice Questions

Q1 Explain how to calculate the mean.
Q2 When is it best not to use the mean?
Q3 What is the difference between the median and the mode?
Q4 Why is the mode sometimes more 'realistic'?
Q5 How is the range calculated?
Q6 What is meant by 'standard deviation'?

Dame Edna Average — making stats fun, possums...

These statistics are used to describe a collection of scores in a data set (how big the scores are, how spread out they are, and so on), so they're called... wait for it... descriptive statistics. Don't be put off by the weirdy maths notation either — a bar on top of a letter (e.g. $\bar{X}$) means you work out the mean. And a sigma (Σ) means you add things up. There... not so bad.

Correlation

You know what they say — correlation is as correlation does.
Remember that as you read this page... then you won't go far wrong.

Correlation Measures How Closely Two Variables are Related

1) **Correlation** is a measure of the relationship between **two variables**, e.g. it would tell you whether exam grades are related to the amount of revision that someone's done.

2) **Correlational studies** are done to collect data for some kind of **correlational analysis**.

The Correlation Coefficient is a Number Between –1 and +1

1) To find the correlation between two variables, you first have to collect some **data**.

   For example, you could ask every student in a class how many hours of study they did each week, and note their average test results.

Student	Hours of study	Average test score — %
A	4	58
B	1	23
C	7	67
D	15	89

2) You can then work out a **correlation coefficient** (e.g. Spearman's rho — see next page). This is a number between –1 and +1, and shows:

   (i) **How closely** the variables are linked. This is shown by the **size** of the number — if it's **close** to +1 or –1, then they are **very closely** related, while a smaller number means the relationship is **less strong** (or maybe not there at all if it's close to 0).

   (ii) The **type** of correlation — a **positive** correlation coefficient (i.e. between 0 and +1) means that the variables rise and fall together, while a negative correlation coefficient (i.e. between –1 and 0) means that as one variable rises, the other falls. (See below for more info.)

Correlation is Easy to See on Scatter Graphs

1) **Positive Correlation** — this means that as one variable rises, so does the other (and likewise, if one falls, so does the other).
   Example: hours of study and average test score.
   Correlation coefficient roughly **0.75** (close to +1)

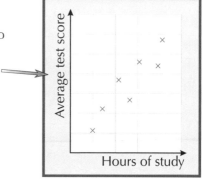

2) **Negative Correlation** — this means that as one variable rises, the other one falls (and vice versa).
   Example: hours of TV watched each week and average test score.
   Correlation coefficient roughly **–0.75** (close to -1).

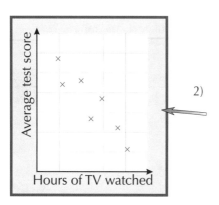

3) **No correlation** — if the correlation coefficient is 0 (or close to 0), then the two variables aren't linked.
   Example: a student's height and their average test score.
   Correlation coefficient roughly **0.01** (close to 0)

Correlation

Correlational Research Has Some Advantages...

1) Because correlational research doesn't involve **controlling** any variables, you can do it when (for **practical** or **ethical** reasons) you couldn't do a **controlled experiment**.

   For example, an experiment into the effects of smoking on humans probably wouldn't be done for ethical reasons, but a correlation between smoking and cancer could be established from hospital records.

2) Correlational analysis can give ideas for **future** research (e.g. biological research on the effects of smoking).

3) Correlation can even be used to test for **reliability** and **validity** (e.g. by correlating the results of the same test taken twice by the same people — a good **reliable** test will show a **high correlation**).

...but some Limitations

1) Correlational analysis **can't** establish 'cause and effect' relationships — it can only show that there's a **statistical link** between them.

   Variables can be closely correlated without one causing the other, for example, when a **third variable** is involved. Only a **controlled experiment** can show cause and effect relationships.

2) Care must be taken when **interpreting** correlation coefficients — high correlation coefficients could be down to **chance**. To decide whether a coefficient is **significant**, you have to use a proper **significance test**.

For example, the number of births in a town was found to be positively correlated to the number of storks that nested in that town — but that didn't mean that more storks caused the increase. (It was because more people in the town led to more births, and also to more houses with chimneys to nest in.)

Spearman's Rho is a Correlation Coefficient

To work out (and then test the significance of) **Spearman's rho** correlation coefficient, you need values for two different variables (e.g. hours of revision and average test scores for 10 students).

a) The values for each variable are placed into **rank order** (each variable is ranked separately). The lowest value for each variable gets rank 1 (and in the above example, the biggest value will get rank 10).

b) The **difference** (**d**) in ranks for each student's variables is calculated. (So a particular student may have done the most revision, but got the 3rd best results, in which case the difference in ranks will be d = 3 – 1 = 2.)

c) The value of d for each student is **squared**, then the results are added together (to get $\sum d^2$).

d) Then the special **Spearman's correlation coefficient** calculation is done, which is $r_s = 1 - \dfrac{6 \times \sum d^2}{N \times (N^2 - 1)}$

   (where N is the number of students, or whatever).

e) To find out whether the result is **significant** (and so whether the variables are linked), you compare the outcome of that nightmarish calculation with a **critical value** that you look up in a **statistics table**.

Practice Questions

Q1 Explain what is meant by correlation.
Q2 What is a correlation coefficient?
Q3 What two things are shown by a correlation coefficient?
Q4 What kind of correlation is shown by a scattergraph whose points start in the upper left and fall to the lower right?
Q5 Explain the difference between a negative correlation and no correlation.
Q6 Describe one use of correlation.

Stats sucks...

Look at the graphs showing the large positive and large negative correlations — all the points lie close-ish to a straight line, which slopes either upwards (positive correlation) or downwards (negative correlation). Just learn the steps involved in working out Spearman's rho — don't try and understand it. Well, that's my advice anyway...

Summarising the Data

It's not very scientific or anything, but the only bit about statistics I don't find mind-numbingly boring is the bit where you get to make all the lovely numbers look pretty... P.S. Ignore me, stats has turned my brain to mush.

Data Can Be Presented in Various Ways

1) **Qualitative** data from observations, interviews, surveys etc (see pages 54-55) can be presented in a **report** as a 'verbal summary'.

2) The report would contain **summaries** of what was seen or said, possibly using **categories** to group data together. Also **quotations** from participants can be used, and any **research hypotheses** that developed during the study or data analysis may be discussed.

3) When **quantitative** data are **collected** (or **produced** from the data, e.g. by a **content analysis** (see page 65), they can be **summarised** and presented in various ways:

Tables are a Good Way to Summarise Quantitative Data

Tables can be used to clearly present the data and show any **patterns** in the scores.

Tables of '**raw data**' show the scores **before** any **analysis** has been done on them.

Other tables may show **descriptive statistics** such as the mean, range and standard deviation (see pages 66-67).

Table To Show the Qualities of Different Types of Ice-cream

Type of ice-cream	Quality (score out of 10)		
	Tastiness	Thickness	Throwability
Chocolate	9	7	6
Toffee	8	6	7
Strawberry	8	5	4
Earwax	2	9	8

Bar Charts Can be used for Non-continuous Data

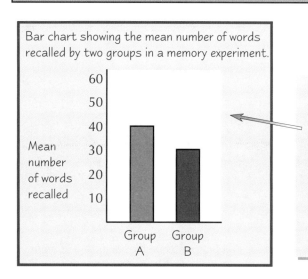

Bar chart showing the mean number of words recalled by two groups in a memory experiment.

Bar charts (bar graphs) are usually used to present '**non-continuous data**' (like when a variable falls into **categories** rather than being measured on a numbered scale).

This bar chart shows the number of words recalled by different groups in a memory experiment.

Note that the columns in bar charts **don't touch** each other. Also, it's preferable to always show the **full vertical scale**, or **clearly indicate** when it isn't all shown (otherwise it can be **misleading**).

Summarising the Data

Nearly done — just a little bit more...

Histograms are For When You Have Continuous Data

Histograms show data measured on a 'continuous' scale of measurement.

This histogram shows the time different participants took to complete a task.

Each column shows a **class interval** (here, each class interval is 10 seconds), and the columns **touch** each other.

It's the **height** of the column that shows the number of values in that interval. (**All** intervals are shown, even if there are **no scores** within it.)

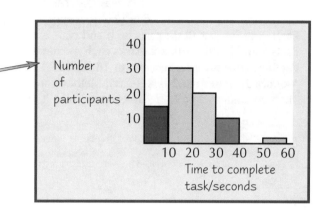

Frequency Polygons are Good For Showing More Than One Set of Data

Frequency polygons are similar to histograms, but use **lines** to show where the top of each column would reach.

It can be useful to combine **two or more** frequency polygons on the same set of axes — then it's easy to **make comparisons** between groups.

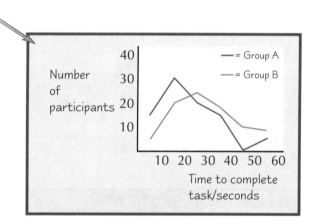

Practice Questions

Q1   How may qualitative data be presented?

Q2   What kind of information is typically shown in tables?

Q3   What kind of data is shown on bar charts?

Q4   Why do the columns on histograms touch?

Q5   What advantage do frequency polygons have over histograms?

What goes 'Graph graph graph'? A dog with a sore throat...*

That's it. It's done. The book is finished. Well, apart from that pesky bit about essays. I think you deserve a big cake now. Go and tell your mum I said so. Say you want one of those really big gooey chocolate ones from the freezer department in the supermarket. And then you'll need a cup of tea too. And a night of watching soap operas and stupid American sit-coms.

* Or a crowd at a tennis match. Or a maths teacher. Or my dad coughing in the morning. Or... oh think of your own...

Do Well in Your Exam

These pages are all about how to do well in AQA A Psychology exams.

Each Module Has 2 Core Areas, Each Made of 2 Questions, Each Made of 3 Parts

1)   **Each** AS module has **two core areas**, e.g. Module 1 has Cognitive Psychology and Developmental Psychology.
2)   **Each core area** has a **choice** of **two questions** — pick one of them.
3)   **Each question** has **three parts** (a, b and c).
4)   **Parts a and b** are worth **six marks each** — they ask you to define terms, describe parts of a study, etc.
5)   **Part c** is an **essay question**, worth **18 marks**.
6)   **Module 3, Core Area 2** is Research Methods and it's a bit **weird**. You get a piece of research described to you. Then you're asked around **7 questions** about it, e.g. identifying variables or interpreting data.

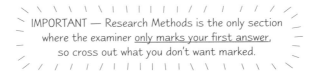

IMPORTANT — Research Methods is the only section where the examiner <u>only marks your first answer</u>, so cross out what you don't want marked.

You Get Marks for *AO1 (knowledge and understanding)* and *AO2 (evaluate and analyse)*

Part a and b questions ask you to demonstrate your **knowledge and understanding** of psychological theories, studies, methods, etc. These are **AO1** marks. You'll be asked to do something like describe a study or explain a term.

Part c questions award 18 marks in total, 6 of which are for **AO1 skills**, the other 12 for **AO2 skills** (so you've got to **evaluate and analyse** psychological theories, studies, etc.)

This means doing things like:

1) presenting **strengths and weaknesses** of a theory/study
2) presenting **alternative** explanations/interpretations of findings
3) using the material to provide a **commentary**, (a well-argued essay).

Here's How to *Do Really Well* in Your Exam:

Firstly, have a look at the **example essay** on the next page.
It shows you the sorts of thing you should remember when you're writing that exam essay.

Secondly, take the advice of our resident expert, Dr Magipoo, famed for his study-coaching:

Study like a nutter or the rabbit gets it.

Do Well in Your Exam

An *Example Essay* to Show You What to Aim at:

"The medical model is the leading approach to dealing with psychological problems."
Describe the biological (medical) model of abnormality and evaluate it in terms of its strengths and weaknesses. (18 marks)

Quotes before essay questions are there to give you ideas — but you can ignore them and just answer the question.

Don't open with a general or meaningless sentence — get straight into gaining marks.

Interpret findings using sentences beginning with 'This suggests that...' etc.

Most AO2 marks will be awarded for your evaluation of strengths and weaknesses — so don't spend too long describing the model.

A02 marks for discussing alternative explanations of findings.

Write a balanced essay by discussing both strengths and weaknesses.

Provide relevant evidence to support the statement.

Don't repeat stuff in the essay, but do put in a conclusion for full marks.

The biological model of abnormality assumes that there is an underlying physiological cause of psychological disorders. Such disorders are considered illnesses just like those which affect the body.

The model includes the idea that genetic factors may be important in psychological disorders. As MZ (identical) twins are 100% genetically identical and DZ (fraternal) twins only share 50% of their genes, MZ twins might be more similar if a condition is inherited. Allen (1976) reported that concordance rates in MZ twins for bipolar disorder are higher than for DZ twins. This suggests that there may be an inherited factor causing bipolar disorder or predisposing someone to the condition.

Another explanation of psychological abnormality is that it is caused by biochemical imbalance. For example, the dopamine hypothesis suggests that excess dopamine may cause schizophrenia. Evidence for this includes the effects of drugs such as amphetamines, which increase dopamine levels and can result in behaviour similar to paranoid schizophrenia. However, an alternative explanation might be that people with schizophrenia are more sensitive to dopamine, rather than they have more of the chemical.

Because the medical model assumes there is a physical cause of abnormality, it uses physical treatments. These include drug therapy (e.g. anti-depressants), electro-convulsive therapy (ECT), which is sometimes used in very severe depression and psychosurgery such as prefrontal lobotomies (used to treat aggressive behaviour).

One strength of this model is that there is evidence supporting the view that there are physical causes underlying some psychological disorders. Krafft-Ebbing (1931) discovered that the psychological condition General Paresis (involving mental deterioration) was caused by the syphilis bacterium. This is an example of an infection, which affects the physical body, being the cause of a psychological disorder.

Physical therapies, such as drugs, have proved effective in treating psychological conditions. Neuroleptic drugs prescribed for schizophrenia are often effective in reducing positive symptoms such as hallucinations and delusions. In some cases, these treatments have enabled people to lead more independent lives. The effectiveness of drugs supports the idea that there are physical causes of psychological conditions.

However, there are problems associated with physical treatments used by this approach. For example, drugs tend to treat symptoms rather than the cause and so do not cure psychological disorders. They may also have serious side effects. Another weakness of the medical model is that there are ethical issues raised by the use of some treatments like ECT. It may be difficult to gain informed consent for treatment from someone with a psychological problem, especially if they don't have insight into the condition. Also, ignoring psychological factors may have negative effects. People may feel more dependent on doctors and take less responsibility for their own psychological well-being.

The medical model has provided evidence that there may be underlying physical causes of psychological disorders. The treatments derived from the approach are often effective, but can have unpleasant side-effects and don't provide a cure. The approach also ignores possible psychological factors that may be involved in psychological disorders. In conclusion, despite its weaknesses, the strengths of the model have maintained its popularity.

Index

Index

Index

Index